The BIG BOOK of LOGOS 3

David E. Carter
Editor

The Big Book of Logos 3

First published in 2002 by HBI,
an imprint of HarperCollins Publishers
10 East 53rd Street
New York, NY 10022-5299

Distributed in the U.S. and Canada by
Watson-Guptill Publications
770 Broadway
New York, NY 10003-9595
Tel: (800) 451-1741
           (732) 363-4511 in NJ, AK, HI
Fax: (732) 363-0338

ISBN: 0-8230-0539-9

Distributed throughout the rest of the world by
HarperCollins International
10 East 53rd Street
New York, NY 10022-5299
Fax: (212) 207-7654

ISBN: 0-06-620940-4

©Copyright 2002 HBI and David E. Carter

All images in this book have been reproduced with the knowledge
and prior consent of the individuals concerned. No responsibility is
accepted by producer, publisher, or printer for any infringement of
copyright or otherwise arising from the contents of this publication.
Every effort has been made to ensure that credits accurately comply
with information supplied.

Printed in Hong Kong by Everbest Printing Company through Four
Colour Imports, Louisville, Kentucky.

Book and jacket design by *Designs on You!*.

By gosh, we've done it again.

First, there was **The Big Book of Logos**. It became a big seller. Actually it became a huge seller.

And so, there was a demand for **The NEW Big Book of Logos**. Same thing. Designers from all over the world discovered that those two books are a great source of inspiration and ideas for logo design.

So they all said: "do it again."

This new **Big Book of Logos**, like the previous two, includes about 2,500 logos, all in full color. And if you design logos, this book (and the other two) really should be at your fingertips.

Why? So you can see what's happening out there in the big world of logo design. There's no larger source than this book (and the other two), and there's no more up-to-date source on logo design than **The Big of Logos 3**.

1.

2.

freerein

3.

4.

5.

6.

7.

8.

4

impli

9.

HEAVENLY STONE

10.

etrieve™

11.

12.

maveron

13.

CHOC

14.

(all)
Design Firm **Hornall Anderson Design Works**

1.
Client	*Care Future*	
Designers	John Hornall, Jana Wilson Esser, Hillary Radbill, Sonja Max, Michael Brugman	

2.
Client	*Seattle Convention & Visitors Bureau*
Designers	Jack Anderson,Lisa Cerveny, Gretchen Cook, Mary Hermes, Michael Brugman, Naomi Davidson, Hillary Radbill, Taka Sakita, Bruce Branson-Meyer, Mark Popich, Don Stayner, Mary Chin Hutchison

3.
Client	*Freerein*
Designers	Jack Anderson, Mark Popich, Tobi Brown, John Anicker, Steffanie Lorig, Bruce Stigler, Ensi Mofasser, Elmer Dela Cruz, John Anderle, Gretchen Cook

4.
Client	*Novell, Inc.*
Designers	Jack Anderson, Larry Anderson, Belinda Bowling, Michael Brugman

5.
Client	*Cougar Mountain Cookies*
Designers	Jack Anderson, Debra McCloskey, Lisa Cerveny, Mary Chin Hutchison, Gretchen Cook, Holly Craven, Dorothee Soechting

6.
Client	*GGLO*
Designers	Debra McCloskey, Steffanie Lorig, Ensi Mofasser, Tobi Brown

7.
Client	*Bucky*
Designers	Jack Anderson, Mary Hermes, Henry Yiu, Gretchen Cook, Elmer Dela Cruz

8.
Client	*Aptimus*
Designers	Jack Anderson, Katha Dalton, Bruce Branson-Meyer, Michael Brugman, Tobi Brown, Mary Hermes, Ed Lee

9.
Client	*Impli*
Designers	Jack Anderson, Kathy Saito, Sonja Max, Alan Copeland

10.
Client	*Heavenly Stone*
Designers	Jack Anderson, Henry Yiu

11.
Client	*etrieve*
Designers	John Hornall, Kathy Saito, Henry Yiu, Alan Copeland, Andrew Smith

12.
Client	*TruckBay*
Designers	Jack Anderson, Debra McCloskey, John Anderle, Andrew Wicklund

13.
Client	*Maveron*
Designers	Jack Anderson, Margaret Long

14.
Client	*CHOC (Children's Hospital of Orange County)*
Designers	Jack Anderson, Lisa Cerveny, Debra McCloskey, Jana Wilson Esser, Jana Nishi, Gretchen Cook, Steffanie Lorig

Photography • Illustration • Whatever

1.

2.

3.

4.

5.

DesignEire

6.

7.

8.

9.

10.

11.

12.

13.

RONDONE ◆ KEMP
CAREER COUNSEL

14.

15.

(all)
Design Firm **Jeff Fisher LogoMotives**
Designer   Jeff Fisher
1.
    Client   *Sam Forencich/SamEyeAm*
    Designer   Jeff Fisher
2.
    Client   *Balloons on Broadway*
    Designer   Jeff Fisher
3.
    Client   *Triangle Productions!*
    Designer   Jeff Fisher
4.
    Client   *Black Dog Furniture Design*
    Designer   Jeff Fisher
    Illustrator Brett Bigham
5.
    Client   *Rose City Softball Association*
6.
    Client   *DesignEire*
    Designers   Jeff Fisher, Nikita Jones
7.
    Client   *DataDork*
    Designer   Jeff Fisher

8.
    Client   *New England Firewood Company*
    Designer   Jeff Fisher
9.
    Client   *Lisa Horne & Family*
    Designer   Jeff Fisher
10.
    Client   *Sisters Rodeo Association*
    Designers   Jeff Fisher, Eloise Boren,
                Sue Fisher (Triad)
11.
    Client   *Rose City Softball Association*
    Designer   Jeff Fisher
12.
    Client   *Portland Fire*
    Designer   Jeff Fisher, Brenda Jacobs
13.
    Client   *Page Six*
    Designer   Jeff Fisher
14.
    Client   *Rondone Kemp*
    Designer   Jeff Fisher
15.
    Client   *Triangle Productions!*
    Designer   Jeff Fisher

1.

2.

3.

4.

5.

6.

7.

8.

9.

10.

11.

12.

13.

14.

Portsmouth Vision 20/20

15.

(all)
Design Firm **Jeff Fisher LogoMotives**
Designer Jeff Fisher
1, 2.
Client *Triangle Productions!*
3.
Client *Aspire Educational Services*
4.
Client *Triangle Productions!*
5.
Client *Balloons on Broadway*
6 - 10.
Client *Triangle Productions!*
11.
Client *WhatNots*
12.
Client *Kimberly Waters*
13.
Client *Triangle Productions!*
14.
Client *KidStuff PR*
15.
Client *Portsmouth Vision 20/20*

1.

2.

3.

4.

5.

6.

7.

1 - 7
Design Firm **Graco Advertising**
1.
   Client   *Graco Industrial Division*
   Designers   Gary Schmidt, Karen Mefford
2.
   Client   *United Way—Internal*
   Designer   Gary Schmidt
3.
   Client   *4 Season Fun Club*
   Designer   Gloria Sheehan
4.
   Client   *Graco CED Division*
   Designers   David Orwoll, Bob Millard
5.
   Client   *Graco Industrial Division*
   Designer   Karen Mefford
6.
   Client   *Graco CED Division*
   Designer   David Orwoll
7.
   Client   *Graco Industrial Division*
   Designer   Gary Schmidt

opposite
   Design Firm **Hornall Anderson Design Works**
   Client   *Bogart Golf*
   Designers   Jack Anderson, James Tee,
                 Henry Yiu, Holly Craven,
                 Mary Chin Hutchison

1.

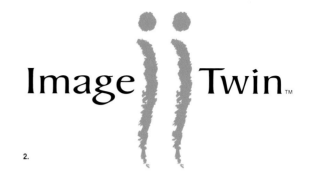

2.

3.

4.

5.

6.

7.

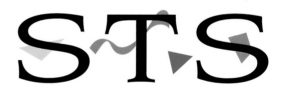

8.

9.

10.

11.

12.

DYNAPAC
P H O T O
Professional Photo Lab

13.

14.

15.

1, 11 - 13, 15
Design Firm **Dynapac Design Group**
2, 4 - 7, 9, 10, 14
Design Firm **Congdon and Company LLC**
3
Design Firm **Graphx Design Seattle**
8
Design Firm **Finished Art, Inc.**

1.
Client   *Exotic Adventures*
Designer   Lee A. Aellig

2.
Client   *Image Twin*
Designers   Nathaniel Brockmann,
            Arthur Congdon

3.
Client   *Gallo Imports & Exports*
Designers   Valerie Forsythe, Patrick Smith,
            Anna Smith

4.
Client   *Ridgefield Community Foundation*
Designer   Arthur Congdon

5.
Client   *Mortgage Sight*
Designer   Nathaniel Brockmann

6.
Client   *STS Jewels*
Designer   Arthur Congdon

7.
Client   *Pepsi Cola*
Designer   Nathaniel Brockmann

8.
Client   *La Tofferie*
Designer   Kannex Fung

9.
Client   *Ocean Connect*
Designers   Nathaniel Brockmann,
            Arthur Congdon

10.
Client   *Pepsi Cola*
Designer   Nathaniel Brockmann

11.
Client   *ZCOR Incorporated*
Designer   Lee A. Aellig

12.
Client   *Lisa Valenzuela*
            Vocal Cords Unlimited
Designer   Lee A. Aellig

13.
Client   *Dynapac Photo*
Designer   Lee A. Aellig

14.
Client   *State of Florida*
Designer   Arthur Congdon

15.
Client   *Caring Angels*
Designer   Lee A. Aellig

1.

2.

3.

4.

PLAZA
EAST
Office
Center

5.

Westport ™

6.

Ca ✈

7.

1 - 7
Design Firm **H2D Incorporated**
1.
Client   *M²*
Designers   Joseph Hausch, Allan Haas
2.
Client   *Outward Focus*
Designers   Joseph Hausch, Terry Lutz
3.
Client   *Johnson Wax*
Designers   Joseph Hausch, Allan Haas
4.
Client   *Vigilo*
Designers   Joseph Hausch, Jennifer Peck
5.
Client   *Plaza East*
Designers   Joseph Hausch, Jennifer Peck
6.
Client   *Bemis Manufacturing*
Designers   Allan Haas, Stacy Slutzky
7.
Client   *Consolidated Aviation*
Designers   Joseph Hausch, Allan Haas,
             Terry Lutz

opposite
Design Firm **1-earth Graphics**
Client   *City of Piqua*
Designer   Lisa Harris

15

1.

2.

3.

4.

5.

6.

7.

8.

من كن الغر بن
AL GHURAIR CENTRE

9.

10.

11.

FLATIRON
MARKETPLACE

12.

Washingtonian Center

14.

13.

VICTORIA
GARDENS

15.

1, 3, 5 - 10, 13, 14
Design Firm **ID8/RTKL Associates Inc.**
2, 4, 11, 12, 15
Design Firm **Redmond Schwartz Design**

1.
Client	*ISLE of CAPRI*
Designers	Thom McKay, Jill Popowich

2.
Client	*Terra Mall*
Designer	Cody Clark

3.
Client	*Seoul Express Terminal Co., LTD.*
Designers	Philips Engelke, Mi Kyung Lee

4.
Client	*Erini Redmond*
Designer	Suzanne Schwartz

5.
Client	*Sonae Imobiliaria SGPS, SA*
Designers	Phil Engelke, Jill Popowich

6.
Client	*CDR Associates*
Designers	Thom McKay, Mi Kyung Lee

7.
Client	*Centros Del Caribe S.A.*
Designers	Phil Engelke, Jill Popowich, Ann Marie Verbrugge

8.
Client	*The Peter Schwartz Foundation*
Designers	Phil Engelke, Jill Popowich, Lynne Barnard

9.
Client	*AL Ghurair Center*
Designers	Phil Engelke, Jill Popowich

10.
Client	*Mitsui Corporation*
Designers	Phil Engelke, Jill Popowich

11.
Client	*The Shops at Tanasbourne*
Designers	D. J. Thomas, Suzanne Schwartz

12.
Client	*Flatiron Marketplace*
Designer	Zuzana Jerieova

13.
Client	*Old Mutual Properties*
Designers	Greg Rose, Young Choe, Phillips Engelke

14.
Client	*The Peterson Companies, LC*
Designers	Phil Engelke, Cindy Reppert, Jill Popowich

15.
Client	*Victoria Gardens*
Designer	D. J. Thomas

1.

2.

3.

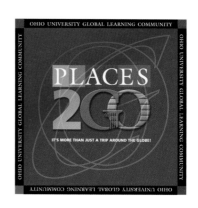

4.

5.

6.

7.

8.

SPEAKEASY
C A S I N O

9.

DERBY ™

28th RUNNING
August 12, 2000

10.

Marble Technologies, Inc.

11.

MTR GAMING GROUP, INC.

12.

SPEEDWAY
CASINO
LAS VEGAS

13.

PRESQUE ISLE DOWNS

14.

LA BONNE VIE
GOURMET RESTAURANT

15.

1 - 8
Design Firm **Ohio University**
9 - 15
Design Firm **Vance Wright Adams
and Associates**

1.
Client *Ohio University*
Designer Mark Krumel
2.
Client *Ohio University*
Designers Mary Dillon, Mark Krumel
3.
Client *Ohio University*
Designers Mary Dillon, Mark Krumel
4.
Client *Ohio University*
Designer Mark Krumel
5.
Client *Ohio University*
Designer Mark Krumel
6.
Client *Ohio University*
Designers Mary Dillon, Mark Krumel

7.
Client *Ohio University*
Designers Mary Dillon, Mark Krumel
8.
Client *Ohio University*
Designer Mark Krumel
9.
Client *MTR Gaming Group, Inc.*
Designers Vance Wright Adams and Associates
10.
Client *Mountaineer Race Track &
Gaming Resort*
Designers Vance Wright Adams and Associates
11.
Client *Marble Technologies, Inc.*
Designers Vance Wright Adams and Associates
12 - 14.
Client *MTR Gaming Group, Inc.*
Designers Vance Wright Adams and Associates
15.
Client *Mountaineer Race Track &
Gaming Resort*
Designers Vance Wright Adams and Associates

1.

dmc²

2.

ROBERT KOCH INSTITUT

3.

ETHYLENE OXIDE · ETHYLENE GLYCOL

EO EG

4.

THE
MARY BAKER EDDY LIBRARY
FOR THE BETTERMENT OF HUMANITY ™

5.

INDIANA
INTERIORS, LLC

6.

7.

1 - 3
Design Firm **MetaDesign**
4, 6
Design Firm **Parsons and Maxson Inc.**
5
Design Firm **Krent / Paffett Associates, Inc.**
7
Design Firm **Gianopoulos Design**
1.
Client   *peace works*
Designers   Uli Mayes, Marion Barbulla,
                  Daniela Hensel, Fabian Rotthe,
                  Jurgen Hubes, Natrin Androschin
2.
Client   *Robert Koch-Institute*
Designers   Marion Burbulla, Fabian Rotthe,
                  Uli Mayes, Daniela Hensel,
                  Jurgen Hubes
3.
Client   *dmc²*
Designers   Erik Spiekesmann,
                  Robert Paulmann

4.
Client   *The Dow Chemical Company*
Designer   Sean Caldwell
5.
Client   *The Mary Baker Eddy Library
                  for the Betterment of Humanity*
Designer   James Silva
6.
Client   *Indiana Interiors, LLC*
Designer   Cynthia Schwannecke
7.
Client   *Albuquerque Arts Alliance*
Designers   Dean Gianopoulos,
                  Tom Antreasian,
                  Kevin Tolman
opposite
Design Firm **X Design Company**
Client   *Ultimate Sailboats*
Designers   Alex Valderrama, Jen Dahlen

ULTIMATE SAILBOATS™

1.

2.

3.

4.

Smart Internet Solutions

5.

6.

7.

8.

22

SOUTHERN MUSEUM OF FLIGHT

9.

DATA DIMENSIONS

10.

11.

12.

GOAHEAD

13.

14.

WHAT WILL YOU
SAVE
TODAY?

15.

23

1.

2.

3.

4.

5.

6.

7.

1 - 4
Design Firm **Becker Design**
5
Design Firm **Bobby Reich-Patri GRAFIX**
6 - 7
Design Firm **Valencia Fine Design**
1.
    Client   *BioForm*
    Designer Neil Becker
2.
    Client   *Beta Systems*
    Designer Neil Becker
3.
    Client   *GreenTree Lending Group*
    Designer Neil Becker
4.
    Client   *Eberhart Interiors*
    Designers Neil Becker, Mary Eich

5.
    Client   *San Francisco Beautiful*
    Designer Bobby Reich-Patri
6.
    Client   *Sun Lion Press*
    Designer Mary Valencia
7.
    Client   *Henning Gutmann—*
                The Gutmann Group
    Designer Mary Valencia
opposite
    Design Firm **AKA Design, Inc.**
    Client   *DB's Sports Bar*
    Designer Mike Mullen

Sports Bar

ST. LOUIS, MO

1.

Setting the Pace

2.

3.

4.

SOUTH SHORE GRILLE
LAKE NORMAN

5. **Simply Catering**

6. **Lids for Kids**

7. RICHIE CUNNINGHAM'S
**Happy Days
Foundation**

8.

26

9.

10.

Jim Gobberdiel Communications

11.

Monsanto People
Leadership Team

12.

13.

generations of hope ®

14.

15.

1 - 8
Design Firm **Phil Evans Graphic Design Inc.**

9, 10
Design Firm **BrandLogic**

11 - 14
Design Firm **Stan Gellman Graphic Design, Inc.**

15
Design Firm **Edelman Financial Services Inc.**

1.
Client *Northeast Medical Center*
Designer Phil Evans

2.
Client *CleanAirClub.Com*
Designer Phil Evans

3.
Client *Phil Evans Graphic Design*
Designer Phil Evans

4.
Client *South Shore Grille*
Designer Phil Evans

5.
Client *Simply Catering*
Designer Phil Evans

6.
Client *WFNZ Sports Radio*
Designer Phil Evans

7.
Client *Happy Days Foundation*
Designer Phil Evans

8.
Client *Lone Star Bowl*
Designer Phil Evans

9.
Client *IBM*
Designer Alfred "Fredy" Jaggi

10.
Client *BrandLogic*
Designer Alfred "Fredy" Jaggi

11.
Client *Jim Gobberdiel Communications*
Designers Barry Tilson, Mike Donovan

12.
Client *Monsanto Company*
Designers Jill Lampen, Teresa Thompson

13.
Client *AHA!*
Designers Mike Donovan, Barry Tilson

14.
Client *Generations of Hope*
Designers Barry Tilson, Erin Goter

15.
Client *The Tavern at Great Falls*
Designer Will Casserly

De La Salle Middle School at St. Matthew's

1.

BIOTECH CONNECTION

You, Monsanto and the World

2.

JOSEPH WU
ORIGAMI INC

3.

ec⚬SPHERES

4.

YESHIVA UNIVERSITY MUSEUM

5.

THEDELI

6.

employee DIRECT WB

7.

1, 2
Design Firm **Stan Gellman Graphic Design, Inc.**
3
Design Firm **Nancy Wu Design**
4
Design Firm **Ron Bartels Design**
5
Design Firm **Barbour Design Inc.**
6
Design Firm **Cramer-Krasselt**
7
Design Firm **Ervin Marketing Creative Communications**

1.
Client *De La Salle Middle School at St. Matthew's*
Designers Barry Tilson, Erin Goter

2.
Client *Monsanto Company*
Designers Teresa Thompson, Jill Lampen, Barry Tilson

3.
Client *Joseph WUOrigami Inc.*
Designer Nancy Wu

4.
Client *Joslyn Castle Institute*
Designer Ron Bartels

5.
Client *Yeshiva University Museum*
Designer Ava Barbour

6.
Client *Pala Casino*
Designers Chris Poisson, Mike Lehnhardt, Anna Wong Yee

7.
Client *Warner Bros.*
Designer Jean Corea

opposite
Design Firm **AKA Design, Inc.**
Client *Object Computing, Inc.—TAO Software*
Designer Mike Mullen

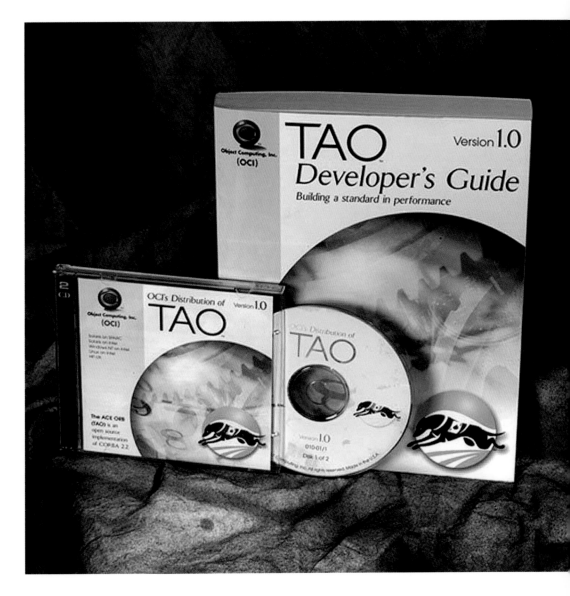

1.

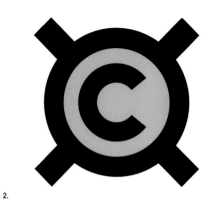

2.

3.

4.

5.

6.

7.

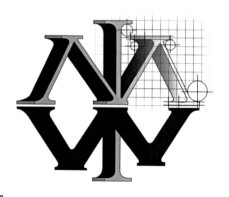

8.

9.

THE GREAT ESCAPE

10.

11.

12.

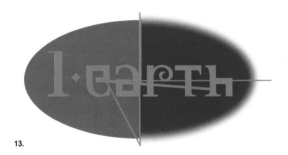

13.

14.

15.

BSI
Bay Systems Integrators

1.

2.

Market!ng
Concepts

3.

4.

Community
CELEBRATION

5.

6.

NAVIGAT⊕R

7.

1 - 3
Design Firm **Jiva Creative**
4, 5
Design Firm **Mona MacDonald Design**
6, 7
Design Firm **Pletka Design**
1.
Client   BSI
Designer   Eric Lee
2.
Client   ArcSource
Designer   Eric Lee
3.
Client   Marketing Concepts
Designer   Eric Lee
4.
Client   eMarket Concepts
Designer   Mona MacDonald
5.
Client   Sisters of St. Joseph
Designer   Mona MacDonald

6.
Client   Nexgen Software
                  Technologies, Inc.
Designer   Diane Pletka
7.
Client   Cova Financial Services
                  Life Insurance
Designers   Diane Pletka, Marie
                  Schrecengost-Carberry
opposite
Design Firm **AKA Design, Inc.**
Client   Kirkwood Parks & Recreation
                  Department
Designer   Stacy Lanier

1.

2.

3.

4.

5.

6.

7.

8.

9.

10.

11.

12.

13.

INDUSTRIES

Contractor's Truss Systems

14.

IKOS

15.

1, 2, 12, 13, 15
Design Firm **Shawver Associates**

3 - 5, 11, 14
Design Firm **Brooks-Jeffrey Marketing, Inc.**

6 - 10
Design Firm **Q. Cassetti**

1.
Client   *123 kids.com*
Designer   Amy Krachenfels

2.
Client   *Weekes Enterprises*
Designer   Kriss Benson

3.
Client   *Buffalo River Cabins*

4.
Client   *Eclectic Eggplant*

5.
Client   *Natco Technologies*

6.
Client   *Corning Museum of Glass*

7.
Client   *Corning Museum of Glass*

8.
Client   *Southeast Steuben County Library*

9.
Client   *Corning Museum of Glass*

10.
Client   *Corning Museum of Glass*

11.
Client   *Custom Cedar*

12.
Client   *Cardoza and Company*
Designer   Marci Dillon

13.
Client   *RIX Industries, Inc.*
Designer   Regina Stadnik

14.
Client   *Contractors' Truss Systems*

15.
Client   *IKOS Systems*
Designers   Mark Shawver, Kyle Ogden,
Teri Gane, Rick Costa, Lily Brady,
Kate McGraw, Marci Dillow

WYOMING
MACHINE

1.

2.

Walker West
Music Academy

Music, the language of the soul.

3.

4.

MINERAL SPRINGS

5.

6.

7.

1, 3, 5
Design Firm **Peggy Lauritsen Design Group**
2
Design Firm **LMS Design**
4
Design Firm **Shea Design**
6
Design Firm **Martin-Schaffer, Inc.**
7
Design Firm **McAdams Group**
1.
Client   *Wyoming Machine*
Designer   John Haines
2.
Client   *DeLorme*
Designer   Richard Shear
3.
Client   *Walker West Music Academy*
Designer   John Haines
4.
Client   *Shea Dairy, Inc.*
Designer   Melissa Shea

5.
Client   *Mineral Springs*
Designer   John Haines
6.
Client   *Black Rock*
Designer   Steve Cohn
7.
Client   *Mustard Seed Ranch*
Designer   Jonathan Mayer
opposite
Design Firm **The Clifford Group**
Client   *Bike Pro-Mobile*
Designer   Brian Clifford

CHIPWRIGHTS

1.

THE MALL AT

STONECREST

ATLANTA

2.

DUWAMISH
**LONGHOUSE
PROJECT**

3.

IMMUNIZE
At All Ages

4.

REDMOND ORTHODONTICS

5.

6.

United
EVANGELICAL FREE CHURCH

7.

TAPROOT THEATRE'S
**NIGHTCAP
IMPROV
COMEDY**

8.

9.

10.

11.

12.

BlueStreak

13.

early arrivals.com

14.

STONEBRIAR
MALL

15.

1, 11, 12, 14
Design Firm **Fassino/Design**
2, 5, 15
Design Firm **Redmond Schwartz Design**
3, 4, 7 - 9
Design Firm **Ray Braun Graphic Design**
6, 10, 13
Design Firm **DesBrow & Associates**

1.
Client *Chipwrights*
Designer Diane Fassino

2.
Client *Stonecrest Mall*
Designer Suzanne Schwartz

3.
Client *Duwamish Tribal Services*
Designer Ray Braun

4.
Client *Washington State Department of Health Immunization Program*
Designer Ray Braun

5.
Client *Redmond Orthodontics*
Designer Suzanne Schwartz

6.
Client *AquaTech, Inc.*
Designer Brian Lee Campbell

7.
Client *United*
Designers Jim Powell, Ray Braun

8.
Client *Taproot Theatre Company*
Designer Ray Braun

9.
Client *King's School*
Designer Ray Braun

10.
Client *Fox Learning Systems- FarSight Brand*
Designer Brian Lee Campbell

11.
Client *Repair, Inc.*
Designers Diane Fassino, Christianne Smith

12.
Client *Sention*
Designer Diane Fassino

13.
Client *Vocollect-BlueStreak Product Identity*
Designer Brian Lee Campbell

14.
Client *Clinician Support Technology*
Designer Diane Fassino

15.
Client *Stonebriar Centre*
Designer Suzanne Schwartz

RUNet 2000

1.

2.

powerpetro

3.

LIVINGSTON COLLEGE

Shaping Our Community

4.

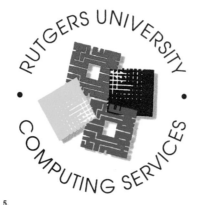

5.

6.

Newman + Cohen

Financial Management

7.

1, 2, 4, 5
Design Firm **Rutgers University**
3, 6, 7
Design Firm **GoldForest**
1.
Client   *RUNet 2000*
Designer   John Van Cleaf
2.
Client   *Center for Neighborhood and Brownfields Redevelopment*
Designer   John Van Cleaf
3.
Client   *PowerPetro, Inc.*
Designer   Sally Ann Field
4.
Client   *Livingston College*
Designer   John Van Cleaf
5.
Client   *Rutgers Computing Services*
Designer   John Van Cleaf

6.
Client   *In-Formation Display Technologies, Inc.*
Designer   Raymond Garcia
7.
Client   *Newman and Cohen*
Designer   Sally Ann Field
opposite
Design Firm **Concrete Design Communications Inc.**
Client   Toronto 2008 Olympic Bid Office
Designer   John Pylypczak

TORONTO

2008

1.

2.

3.

4.

5.

6.

BUCKLE DOWN
CLEVELAND

Cuyahoga County Safety Belt Program

7.

8.

9.

10.

11.

A SHEAR ENCOUNTER LTD
SALON & DAY SPA

12.

13.

14.

15.

PEZ LAKE DEVELOPMENT LLC

1.

TANDOORI NIGHTS

2.

Jungle PARTY

3.

The Getaway Lounge

4.

Baltisse ™

5.

SAGEWORTH

6.

Rhapsody in Blue ™

7.

1, 2, 4,
Design Firm **Levine & Assoc.**
3
Design Firm **Graphica Communication Solutions**
5 - 7
Design Firm **Albert Bogner Design Communications**

1.
Client *Pez Lake Development*
Designer Lena Markley

2.
Client *Tandoori Nights*
Designer Monica Snellings

3.
Client *Woodland Park Zoo*
Designer Robin Walker

4.
Client *St. Peter's Interparish School*
Designer Monica Snellings

5.
Client *Baltisse*
Designers Kelly Albert, Marie Elaina Miller

6.
Client *Sageworth*
Designer Kelly Albert

7.
Client *Nissley Vineyard*
Designer Marie Elaina Miller

opposite
Design Firm **Redmond Schwartz Design**
Client *The Promenade in Temecula*
Designers D.J. Thomas, Suzanne Schwartz

1.

Audubon Nature Institute
Celebrating the Wonders of Nature

2.

Y YMCA
OF GREATER NEW YORK

150
Y E A R S
1852 - 2002

3.

PRECARE
for Babies
GIVING YOUR BABY THE BEST START

4.

WILLIAM & SARAH LAWRENCE SOCIETY

5.

6.

THE
LEARNING
ACADEMY

Knowledge to Succeed

7.

8.

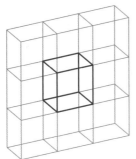

TheSquare.com

The Power of Your Network.
Squared.

9.

10.

11.

Celebrating Rural
Georgia

12.

ITi

13.

F/ST TIDE

14.

Walk A Mile
In My Shoes

15.

1, 11, 13
Design Firm **GOLD & Associates**
2, 4, 15
Design Firm **Porter Novelli**
3, 5, 6, 9, 14
Design Firm **Suka & Friends Design, Inc.**
7, 12
Design Firm **Georgia System Operations Corp.**
8, 10
Design Firm **Brent M. Almond**

1.
Client *South Orange Performing Arts Center*
Designers Peter Butcavage, Joe Vavra, Keith Gold
2.
Client *Audubon Nature Institute*
Designers Penny Rigler, Peter Buttecali
3.
Client *YMCA of Greater New York*
Designer Brian Wong
4.
Client *PreCare*
Designers Penny Rigler, Melissa Whitco
5.
Client *Sarah Lawrence College*
Designer Brian Wong

6.
Client *Barry Gordin Photography*
Designer Gwen Haberman
7.
Client *Oglethorpe Power Corporation*
Designer Brian Rickmond
8.
Client *Kelleen Griffin*
Designer Brent M. Almond
9.
Client *The Square.com*
Designer Sean Garretson
10.
Client *David Marcus*
Designer Brent M. Almond
11.
Client *Life Messages, Inc.*
Designers Keith Gold, Peter Butcavage
12.
Client *Oglethorpe Power Economic Development*
Designer Harry Ankeny
13.
Client *I. T. I. Marketing, Inc.*
Designers Keith Gold, Peter Butcavage
14.
Client *Fasttide*
Designer Sean Garretson
15.
Client *Children's Hospital*
Designer Penny Rigler

47

CONSUMER DATABASE
DQi³

1.

Eagle Alliance

2.

3.

D-ONE
IN REAL TIME

4.

BRANDABLE™

5.

24 7 REFERENCE

6.

PARIS '01
CSC

7.

1, 4
　　Design Firm **G2 Alliance**
2, 7
　　Design Firm **P-2 Communications
　　　　　　　 Services Computer Sciences
　　　　　　　 Corporation**
3
　　Design Firm **Kontrapunkt**
5, 6
　　Design Firm **Zyrex, Inc.**
1.
　　Client　　　*Donnelley Marketing*
　　Designer　 Larry Teolis
2.
　　Client　　　*Computer Sciences*
　　Designer　 Bryn Farrar
3.
　　Client　　　*Kontrapunkt (Slovenia)*
　　Designer　 Eduard cehovin
4.
　　Client　　　*Donnelley Marketing*
　　Designer　 Larry Teolis

5.
　　Client　　　*Brandable*
　　Designer　 Erika Kao
6.
　　Client　　　*Metropolitan Cooporative
　　　　　　　　 Library System*
　　Designer　 Erika Kao
7.
　　Client　　　*P-2 Communications Services
　　　　　　　　 Computor Sciences Corporation*
　　Designer　 Francois Fontaine
opposite
　　Design Firm **Concrete Design
　　　　　　　 Communications Inc.**
　　Client　　　*Hydro One*
　　Designer　 John Pylypczak

1.

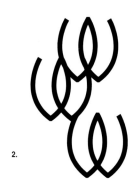

2.

SHU UEMURA BOUTIQUE'S BIRTHDAY

3.

PACHAMAMA'S
NEW WORLD CUISINE

4.

5.

RECORDSCENTER.COM

6.

7.

8.

9.

10.

11.

INTOUCH
SOLUTIONS

12.

13.

14. *Petite Loutre*

Squiggles and Giggles
Fun art for kids!

15.

1.

2.

Ruetschle Architects

3.

nurturing nature

4.

firefly
BUILDING

5.

ATHLETES in action

6.

Miss Behavin

7.

1 - 7
Design Firm **Visual Marketing Associates, Inc.**

1.
Client   *Epic International*
Designers   Joel P. Warneke, Greg Fehrenbach

2.
Client   *Airborne Bicycles*
Designers   Greg Fehrenbach, Joel Warneke

3.
Client   *John Ruetschle Associates*
Designers   Amy Baas, Steven Goubeaux

4.
Client   *Wegerzyn Children's Garden*
Designers   Amy Baas, Kenneth Botts

5.
Client   *Cre8ive Dayton*
Designers   Kenneth Botts, Jen Dutcher, Al Hidalgo

6.
Client   *Athletes In Action*
Designers   Steven Goubeaux, Al Hidalgo

7.
Client   *Airborne Bicycles*
Illustrator   Joel Warneke
Typographer Greg Fehrenbach

opposite
Design Firm **Indiana Design Consortium, Inc.**
Client   *Spectrum Technologies, Inc.*
Designer   Debra Pohl Green

KEEPING YOU ORGANIZED

1.

2.

imaginative solutions.

with Kathaleen Hanna

3.

THE chamber music society of MINNESOTA

4.

THE UNIVERSITY OF TOLEDO

5.

Seattle Architectural Foundation

6.

Seattle Architectural Foundation

7.

Seattle Architectural Foundation

8.

9.

10.

11.

12.

13.

14.

15.

1, 4, 10 - 12, 15
Design Firm **Tilka Design**

2, 6 - 9
Design Firm **Michael Courtney Design**

3, 5, 13, 14
Design Firm **Hoeck Associates, Inc.**

1.
Client   Smead

2.
Client   Fleischmann Office Interiors
Designers   Mike Courtney, Dan Hoang,
             Heidi Favour, Brian O'Neill

3.
Client   VT Entertainment
Designer   Marcia Hoeck

4.
Client   The Chamber of Music Society
Designer   Sarah Steil

5.
Client   The University of Toledo
Designers   Linda Szyskowski, Rosie Boger,
             Diane Ball

6, 7, 8.
Client   Seattle Architectural Foundation
Designers   Mike Courtney, Scott Souchock,
             Dan Hoang
Photographer
             Ted Grudowski

9.
Client   Vulcan Northwest
             (505 Union Station)
Designers   Mike Courtney, Scott Souchock

10.
Client   hk portfolio
Designer   Shannon Shriver

11.
Client   GTCYS
Designer   Tamatha Schneider

12.
Client   MCCA (Mississippi Corridor
             Community Alliance)
Designer   Micheal Wallner

13.
Client   VT Entertainment
Designer   Linda Szyskowski

14.
Client   Junior League/Toledo Chapter
Designers   Marcia Hoeck, Linda Szyskowski,
             Diane Ball

15.
Client   Imation

3.

1.

5.

7.

2.

4.

6.

1 - 7
Design Firm **Zunda Design Group**
1.
Client   *Tear of the Clouds, LLC*
Designers   Todd Nickel, Charles Zunda
2.
Client   *B+G Foods, Inc.*
Designer   Charles Zunda
3.
Client   *New England Brewing Company*
Designers   Todd Nickel, Charles Zunda
4.
Client   *Newman's Own Inc.*
Designers   Charles Zunda, Todd Nickel,
                 Maija Riekstins
5.
Client   *Playtex Products, Inc.*
Designers   Todd Nickel, Charles Zunda
6.
Client   *World Finer Foods, Inc.*
Designers   Todd Nickel, Charles Zunda
7.
Client   *GAA Corporation*
Designer   Todd Nickel

opposite
Design Firm **Zunda Design Group**
Client   *GAA Corporation*
Designer   Todd Nickel

The ORIGINAL Shows from Radio's Most Famous Western

5 COMPACT DISCS

56 PAGE BOOK

THE LONE RANGER CHRONICLES

LIMITED COLLECTOR'S SET EDITION

A fiery horse with the speed of light, a cloud of dust and a hearty "Hi-Yo, Silver"

1.

PLISE DEVELOPMENT & CONSTRUCTION

2.

3.

4.

5.

6.

7.

8.

9.

10.

11.

brand.™

12.

13.

redHookreads

14.

15.

1.

2.

3.

4.

5.

6.

7.

1 - 3
Design Firm **INC 3**
4 - 7
Design Firm **Wages Design**
1.
    Client   *Elara Diamonds*
    Designers   Harvey Appelbaum,
                Steve Swingler
2.
    Client   *Centurion Jewelry*
    Designers   Harvey Appelbaum,
                Steve Swingler
3.
    Client   *Internet Services Center*
    Designers   Harvey Appelbaum,
                Christopher Nystrom
4.
    Client   *ObjectStorm*
    Designer   Diane Kim
5.
    Client   *UPC (Utilities Protection Center)*
    Designer   Matt Taylor

6.
    Client   *Arris*
    Designer   Joanna Tak
7.
    Client   *AIGA Big Night (Atlanta)*
    Designer   Dominga Lee
opposite
    Design Firm **Zunda Design Group**
    Client   *Playtex Products, Inc.*
    Designers   Todd Nickel, Charles Zunda

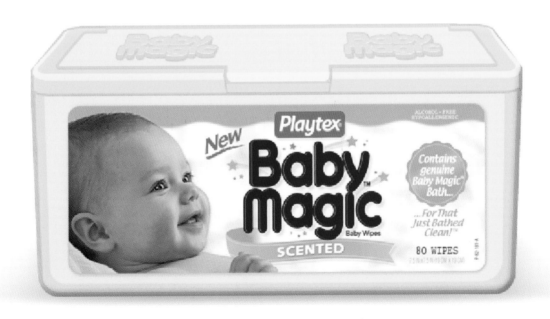

1.

2.

3.

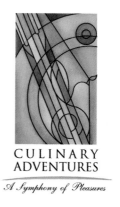

4.

5.

CULINARY
ADVENTURES
A Symphony of Pleasures

6.

7.

8.

9.

10.

11.

12.

13.

14.

15.

1.

2.

3.

4.

5.

6.

7.

1 - 3
Design Firm **Stephen Loges Graphic Design**
4
Design Firm **VNO**
5
Design Firm **The Creative Mind**
6, 7
Design Firm **Basler Design Group**
1.
  Client   *New Leaf Career Solutions*
  Designer Stephen Loges
2.
  Client   *BioNexus Foundation*
  Designer Stephen Loges
3.
  Client   *Jim Barber Studio/ Electric Stock*
  Designer Stephen Loges
4.
  Client   *Guitarded*
  Designer Jim Vienneau

5.
  Client   *Team Voodoo Cycling Club*
  Designer Dan Schuster
6.
  Client   *Steadyhold*
  Designers Dan Schuster, Bill Basler
7.
  Client   *Phelan's Interiors*
  Designers Bill Basler, Drew Davies
opposite
  Design Firm **Harbauer Bruce Nelson Design**
  Client   *Ace Hardware*
  Designer Larry Teolis

1.

2.

3.

4.

5.

6.

7.

8.

9.

VISUALSOLUTIONS

10.

11.

FiSHBONE

SEAFOOD MARKET & GRILL

12.

Serving Contemporary Nostalgia

14.

13.

CIBOLA

15.

1, 3 - 6, 9, 12, 14,		
Design Firm **Unigraphics, Inc.**		
2, 7, 8, 10, 11, 13, 15		
Design Firm **Gardner Design**		

1.
Client *Michael Jenkins*
Designers Jack Evans, Bonnie Evans, Clay McClure

2.
Client *Plazago*
Designer Bill Gardner

3.
Client *K•DO*
Designers Jack Evans, Bonnie Evans, Clay McClure

4.
Designers Jack Evans, Bonnie Evans, Clay McClure

5.
Client *Gerry Angeli*
Designers Jack Evans, Bonnie Evans, Clay McClure

6.
Client *Michael Ruff*
Designers Jack Evans, Bonnie Evans, Clay McClure

7.
Client *Hoch Haus*
Designer Bill Gardner

8.
Client *Balance*
Designer Brian Miller

9.
Client *Paul Morrisey*
Designers Jack Evans, Bonnie Evans, Clay McClure

10.
Client *Vizworx*
Designer Bill Gardner

11.
Client *Saffelli Coffee House*
Designer Travis Brown

12.
Client *Ed Cervantes*
Designers Jack Evans, Bonnie Evans, Clay McClure

13.
Client *Safe Temp*
Designer Chris Parks

14.
Client *Jim Duda*
Designers Jack Evans, Bonnie Evans, Clay McClure

15.
Client *Cibola*
Designer Chris Parks

1.

2.

3.

4.

5.

6.

7.

1.

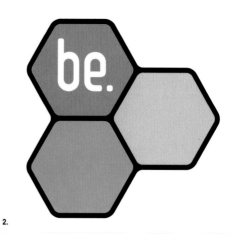

2.

NORS

3.

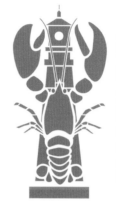

4.

CRESTVIEW
PLAZA

5.

corrigo

6.

BRIAN
OLSON
MEMORIAL
GOLF CLASSIC

7.

1, 3, 4,
Design Firm **Jasper & Bridge Assoc.**
2, 6, 7
Design Firm **be.design**
5
Design Firm **Gardner Design**

1.
  Client   *Michael Charek Architects*
  Designer Kim Noyes
2.
  Client   *be.design*
  Designers Eric Read, Yusuke Asaka,
             Will Burke
3.
  Client   *Nors Sport*
  Designer Alexander Bridge
4.
  Client   *New England American
             Institute of Architects*
  Designer Kim Noyes
5.
  Client   *Crestview Plaza*
  Designer Bill Gardner

6.
  Client   *Corrigo*
  Designers Eric Read, Yusuke Asaka,
             Will Burke
7.
  Client   *Brian Olson Memorial
             Golf Classic*
  Designers Eric Read, Yusuke Asaka,
             Will Burke
opposite
  Design Firm **Indiana Design
                Consortium, Inc.**
  Client   *Spectrum Technologies, Inc.*
  Designers Debra Pohl Green, Steve Miller

FIELD SCOUT™
Chlorophyll Meter

1.

2.

3.

4.

5.

6.

7.

1, 2, 4, 6, 7
Design Firm **Gardner Design**
3
Design Firm **Dever Designs**
5
Design Firm **PA2 Design Group**

1.
Client   *Virtual Focus*
Designer   Chris Parks

2.
Client   *Richmond Raceway*
Designer   Travis Brown

3.
Client   *Development Alternatives Inc.*
Designer   Jeffrey L. Dever

4.
Client   *Fidel Bistro*
Designer   Travis Brown

5.
Client   *Carlton Plants*
Designer   Von R. Glitschka

6.
Client   *Buzz Cuts Maximum Lawncare*
Designer   Bill Gardner

7.
Client   *Somnograph*
Designers   Bill Gardner, Brian Miller

opoosite
Design Firm **be.design**
Client   *Cost Plus World Market*
Designers   Eric Read, Coralie Russo

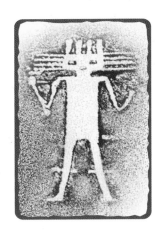

ATACAMA

1.

2.

3

4.

5.

6.

7.

8.

PIVOTAL
TRAINING CENTER

9.

10.

SEACLIFF

11.

12.

Mr SWAP.COM

13.

14.

15.

1, 11 - 13
Design Firm **be.design**
2, 3, 6, 7, 9, 10, 14
Design Firm **Gardner Design**
4, 5, 15
Design Firm **Espy Graphics**
8
Design Firm **Paz Design Group**

1.
Client — *Microsoft*
Designers — Eric Read, Yusuke Asaka, Will Burke

2.
Client — *Bredar Waggoner Architecture*
Designer — Travis Brown

3.
Client — *Donovan Transit*
Designer — Travis Brown

4.
Client — *Upper Deck Company*
Designer — Von R. Glitschka

5.
Client — *Fire Giant*
Designer — Von R. Glitschka

6.
Client — *CRC*
Designer — Chris Parks

7.
Client — *Whoburt N. Winchester*
Designer — Chris Parks

8.
Client — *Elsinore Theatre*
Designer — Von R. Glitschka

9.
Client — *Pivotal*
Designers — Chris Parks, Travis Brown

10.
Client — *Virtual Focus*
Designer — Chris Parks

11.
Client — *Cost Plus World Market*
Designers — Eric Read, Diane Hilde, Will Burke

12.
Client — *Digiscents*
Designers — Eric Read, Yusuke Asaka, Coralie Russo, Will Burke

13.
Client — *Mr. Swap*
Designers — Eric Read, Yusuke Asaka, John Meeks

14.
Client — *Burke Corporation*
Designers — Bill Gardner, Dave LaFleur

15.
Client — *Seventh Millennium*
Designer — Von R. Glitschka

GOVERNOR NELSON A. ROCKEFELLER
EMPIRE STATE PLAZA

1.

2.

D▤LT▲G▲

CONTINENTAL CAFE

3.

RUNNING WITH SCISSORS

4.

ARES

5.

CEƏ3

6.

Kansas Joint Replacement Institute

7.

1, 3
Design Firm **The Hillier Group**
2, 5, 7
Design Firm **Gardner Design**
4, 6
Design Firm **Richard Zeid Design**
1.
Client   *State of New York Office*
    of General Services
Designers   John Bosio, Despina Raggousis
2.
Client   *Prairie Fest*
Designers   Brian Miller, Bill Gardner
3.
Client   *Astra-Merck*
Designers   John Bosio, Susan Wisniewski
4.
Client   *Running with Scissors*
Designer   Richard Zeid

5.
Client   *ARES*
Designer   Chris Parks
6.
Client   *CEE3 Design*
Designer   Richard Zeid
7.
Client   *KJRI*
Designer   Bill Gardner
opposite
Design Firm **Arnell Group**
Client   *Rockport*
Designer   Peter Arnell

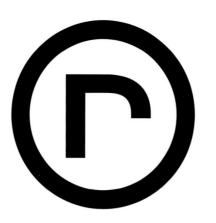

ROCKPORT

1.

2.

3.

4.

5.

6.

7.

8.

9.

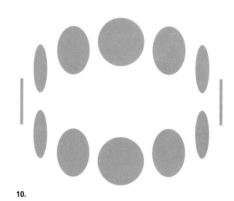

10.

11.

12.

13.

SPREE '01

14.

15.

1, 4, 8, 11, 12, 14, 15
Design Firm **Graphx Design Seattle**
2, 9, 10,
Design Firm **Gee & Chung Design**
3, 5 - 7, 13,
Design Firm **Laura Manthey Design**

1.
Client — *Hiatt Construction*
Designers — Anna Smith, Valerie Forsythe
2.
Client — *Alliance Healthcare Foundation*
Designers — Earl Gee, Fani Chung
3.
Client — *PPONEXT*
Designer — Laura Manthey
4.
Client — *Y.K. Products*
Designers — Patrick Smith, Alex Sobie
5.
Client — *Sweet Earth*
Designer — Laura Manthey
6.
Client — *Financial Architect*
Designer — Laura Manthey
7.
Client — *McCaffrey Root Beer*
Designer — Laura Manthey

8.
Client — *Newport Seafoods, Inc.*
Designers — Patrick Smith, Valerie Forsythe
9.
Client — *Bay Area Air Quality Management District*
Designer — Earl Gee
10.
Client — *Art Center College of Design Alumni Council*
Designer — Earl Gee
11.
Client — *Game Factory*
Designers — Anna Smith, Valerie Forsythe
12.
Client — *Silhouette*
Designers — Patrick Smith, Alex Sobie, Valerie Forsythe
13.
Client — *Squeeze Play*
Designer — Laura Manthey
14.
Client — *Seattle Preparatory High School*
Designers — Patrick Smith, Valerie Forsythe
15.
Client — *Zebra Solutions*
Designers — Valerie Forsythe, Anna Smith

1.

2.

3.

4.

5.

6.

7.

1.

2.

IRONWORKERS • PRESS BRAKES • SHEARS

PRAIRIE
STATE • BANK

3.

eden
Promotions
Advertising Incentives & Promotional Merchandise

4.

WICHITA
festivals inc

5.

6.

Brandology
Marketing Consulting

7.

mom 'n' me designs
Gift Baskets for all occasions

8.

9.

10.

11.

12.

13.

14.

15.

1, 2, 3, 5, 10, 12
Design Firm **Gardner Design**
4, 6, 8, 9, 13, 14
Design Firm **Gabriella Sousa Designs**
7, 15
Design Firm **Design Directions**
11
Design Firm **DeMartino Design**

1.
Client	*Burke Corporation*
Designers	Bill Gardner, Dave LaFleur

2.
Client	*Piranha*
Designer	Chris Parks

3.
Client	*Prairie State Bank*
Designer	Chris Parks

4.
Client	*Eden Promotions*
Designer	Gabriella Sousa

5.
Client	*Wichita Festivals, Inc.*
Designer	Bill Gardner

6.
Client	*Brooklyn's Restaurant*
Designer	Gabriella Sousa

7.
Client	*Brandology*
Designers	Melissa Muldoon, Maura Mitchell

8.
Client	*Mom 'n' me Designs*
Designer	Gabriella Sousa

9.
Client	*Computechniques*
Designer	Gabriella Sousa

10.
Client	*Burke Corporation*
Designers	Bill Gardner, Dave LaFleur

11.
Client	*Chemical Bank*
Designer	Erick DeMartino

12.
Client	*Pratt Regional Medical Center*
Designer	Chris Parks

13.
Client	*Calliope Sound Productions*
Designer	Gabriella Sousa

14.
Client	*Kidzexchange.com*
Designer	Gabriella Sousa

15.
Client	*Siena Analytics*
Designer	Melissa Muldoon

1.

MAY 6th, 1998

2.

3.

4.

5.

6

7.

1, 4
Design Firm **Karacters Design Group**
2, 5, 7
Design Firm **Articulation Group**
3, 6
Design Firm **Gardner Design**

1.
Client   *McDonald's*
Designers   Maria Kennedy,
            Michelle Melenchuk
2.
Client   *Highland Feather*
Designer   Joseph Chan
3.
Client   *Big Fish*
Designer   Chris Parks
4.
Client   *Caboodles Cosmetics*
Designers   Maria Kennedy,
            Michelle Melenchuk
5.
Client   *Internac*
Designer   Joseph Chan

6.
Client   *Allen's Excavating*
Designer   Chris Parks
7.
Client   *Youth Challenge*
            International
Designers   Joseph Chan,
            David Drummond

opposite
Design Firm **Concrete Design**
            Communications Inc.
Client   *Umbra*
Designers   Claire Dawson,
            John Pylypczak

umbra

1.

2.

3.

4.

5.

6.

7.

8.

9.

10.

11.

12.

13.

14.

SJOBERG ❦ TEBELIUS
ATTORNEYS & COUNSELORS
AT LAW

15.

1, 2, 4, 11
Design Firm **GCG**
3, 7, 13 - 15
Design Firm **Resco Print Graphics**
5, 6, 8 - 10, 12
Design Firm **Art O Mat Design**

1.
Client | McBee Homes
Designer | Brian Wilburn

2.
Client | XTO Energy
Designer | Brian Wilburn

3.
Client | River Falls Area
 | Chamber of Commerce
Designers | Hattie Thornton,
 | Trudy Whitemire

4.
Client | Expansa
Designer | Brian Wilburn

5.
Client | NW Member Network
Designers | Jacki McCarthy, Mark Kaufman

6.
Client | Greater Seattle
 | Chamber of Commerce
Designers | Jacki McCarthy, Mark Kaufman

7.
Client | St. Croix Trading
Designer | Sandy Plank
Illustrator | Mark Carey

8, 9.
Client | Sports and Events Council
 | of Seattle/King County
Designers | Jacki McCarthy, Mark Kaufman

10.
Client | The Rocket
Designers | Jacki McCarthy, Mark Kaufman

11.
Client | Mark Brooks Golf
Designer | Brian Wilburn

12.
Client | Sports and Events Council
 | of Seattle/King County
Designers | Jacki McCarthy, Mark Kaufman

13.
Client | Raleigh Cycle Service
Designer | Sandy Plank

14.
Client | House Calls
Designer | Barb Smothers

15.
Client | Sjoberg & Tebelius
Designer | Trudy Whitmire

1.

2.

SMARTEGG
LEGACY

3.

4.

5.

6.

Piller's ®

7.

1
Design Firm **Bryan Friel**
2, 3, 5 - 7
Design Firm **Articulation Group**
4
Design Firm **Green Springs Cafe**
1.
   Client   *It's a Grind*
   Designers Bryan Friel, Marty Cox
2.
   Client   *Creative Performance*
   Designers Joseph Chan, Karin Fukuzawa
3.
   Client   *Smart Egg*
   Designer   Joseph Chan
4.
   Client   *Green Springs Cafe*
   Designer   Kris Kubik
5.
   Client   *Royal Bank of Canada*
   Designer   Joseph Chan

6.
   Client   *Community Express*
   Designer   Joseph Chan
7.
   Client   *Piller's*
   Designer   Joseph Chan
opposite
   Design Firm **Interflow**
               Communications Ltd.
   Client   *Pepsi Pakistan*

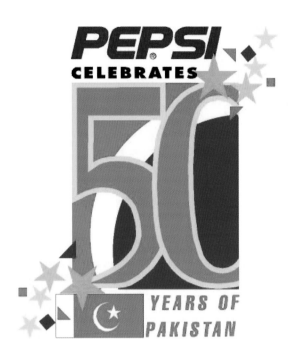

1.

2.

3.

4.

5.

6.

7.

8.

Save the Children's Studio
F U N D R A I S E R

9.

10.

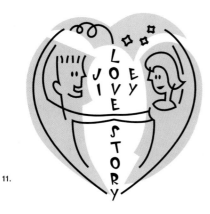

JOY
LOVELY
STORY

11.

caboodles®

12.

Power of 4

13.

www.barqs.com

14.

saving**u**money.com™

15.

1.

2.

three + associates

3.

4.

ATRIUM
cafe

5.

LAND OF OZ

6.

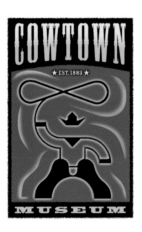

7.

1, 2, 4, 6, 7
Design Firm **Gardner Design**
3
Design Firm **Three & Associates**
5
Design Firm **Lidia Varesco Design**
1.
Client   *Chef's Pride*
Designer   Brian Miller
2.
Client   *Blue Hat Media*
Designer   Chris Parks
3.
Client   *Three & Associates*
Designers   Chris Miller, Gordon Cotton
4.
Client   *Gavin Peters Photo*
Designer   Travis Brown
5.
Client   *Levy Restaurants/*
           Indian Lakes Resort
Designer   Lidia Varesco

6.
Client   *Land of Oz*
Designer   Travis Brown
7.
Client   *Cowtown Museum*
Designer   Travis Brown
opposite
Design Firm **Sayles Graphic Design**
Client   *Christopher's*
Designer   John Sayles

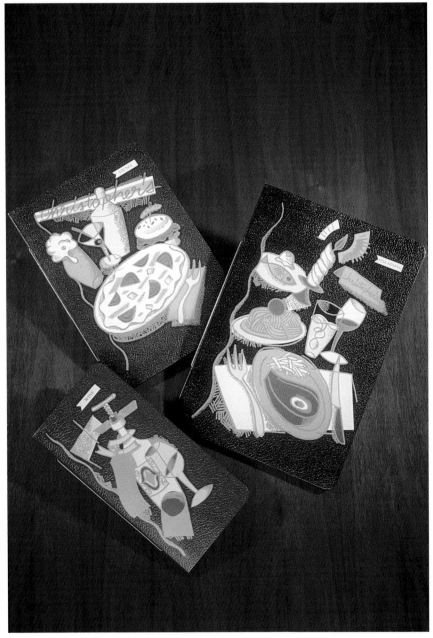

1.

2.

The Kids' Division of Brown Shoe

3.

4.

5.

6.

7.

8.

9.

10.

11.

ProperCare™

12.

CHILDREN'S ZOO

13.

14.

15.

1.

2.

3.

4.

5.

6.

7.

1 - 3, 7
Design Firm **Capstone Studios Inc.**
4, 6
Design Firm **Kiku Obata & Company**
5
Design Firm **Nancy Stentz Design**
1.
Client   *Ed Segura/*
             Double Eagle Casino
Designers   John Taylor Dismukes,
             JoAnne Redwood
2.
Client   *Big Inc./Steve Miles*
Designers   John Taylor Dismukes,
             JoAnne Redwood
3.
Client   *Adexd/Vista 2001*
Designers   John Taylor Dismukes,
             JoAnne Redwood

4.
Client   *River Park Square*
Designer   Scott Gericke
5.
Client   *University of California/*
             School of Arts
Designer   Nancy Stentz
6.
Client   *Brown Shoe Company*
Designers   Scott Gericke, Amy Knopf,
             Joe Floresca, Jennifer Baldwin
7.
Client   *McGraw Hill Publication*
Designers   John Taylor Dismukes,
             JoAnne Redwood,
             Jeanne Schacht
opposite
Design Firm **Sayles Graphic Design**
Client   *2000 Iowa State Fair "Zero In"*
Designer   John Sayles

1.

2.

3.

4.

5.

6.

7.

8.

9.

10.

11.

12.

13.

14.

15.

1 - 6
Design Firm **Kiku Obata & Company**
7 - 10
Design Firm **Capstone Studios Inc.**
11 - 13
Design Firm **DeLisle & Associates**
14, 15
Design Firm **Rickabaugh Graphics**
1 - 6.
Client   *St. Louis Zoo*
Designer   Rich Nelson
7.
Client   *Victoria Hart/Westwood Studios*
Designers   John Taylor Dismukes,
             JoAnne Redwood
8.
Client   *Art Tech International*
Designers   John Taylor Dismukes,
             JoAnne Redwood
9.
Client   *Andy Crews/Paramont Parks*
Designers   John Taylor Dismukes,
             JoAnne Redwood

10.
Client   *Hoshizaki Ice Machines*
Designers   John Taylor Dismukes,
             JoAnne Redwood
11.
Client   *Disney Cruise Line*
Designers   Tim DeLisle, Jack Crouse III
12, 13.
Client   *Disney Cruise Line*
Designer   Jack Crouse III
14, 15.
Client   *Hampton University*
Designers   Eric Rickabaugh, Dave Cap

1.

2.

3.

4.

LAFAYETTE MAYOR'S
YOUTH COUNCIL

5.

brillhart**media**

6.

7.

1
  Design Firm **Arcanna, Inc.**
2, 7
  Design Firm **Articulation Group**
3
  Design Firm **Seasonal Specialties**
4
  Design Firm **Fixgo Advertising Sdn Bhd**
5
  Design Firm **Indiana Design Consortium, Inc.**
6
  Design Firm **Dever Designs**
1.
  Client   *Bonjour: La Parisienne*
  Designer Sandra Schoultz
2.
  Client   *Solect*
  Designer Joseph Chan
3.
  Client   *Seasonal Specialties*
  Designer Tracy Olson

4.
  Client   *EON Rally*
  Designer FGA Creative Team
5.
  Client   *City of Lafayette*
  Designer Kristy Blair
6.
  Client   *Brillhart Media*
  Designer Jeffrey L. Dever
7.
  Client   *Coors Light*
  Designer Joseph Chan
opposite
  Design Firm **Evenson Design Group**
  Client   *54th Little League World
             Series 2000*
  Designers Mark Sojka, Rose Hartono
  Illustrator Wayne Watford

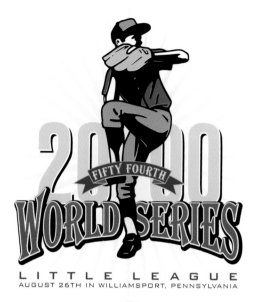

1.

learning.com

2.

3.

FIVE STAR PROPERTIES

4.

5.

6.

7.

8.

9.

10.

11.

13.

12.

KEN LeGROS
Photography

14.

P A R K L O F T

15.

1, 3 - 5, 7
Design Firm **The Wecker Group**
2, 6, 8, 9, 14
Design Firm **Dotzero Design**
10 - 13, 15
Design Firm **Sabingrafik, Inc.**

1.
Client　　　*John Saar Properties*
Designer　　Robert Wecker

2.
Client　　　*Learning.com*
Designers　 Karen Wippich, Jon Wippich

3.
Client　　　*Monterey Bay Printing*
Designers　 Robert Wecker, Matt Gnibus

4.
Client　　　*Five Star Properties*
Designer　　Robert Wecker

5.
Client　　　*Fasback*
Designers　 Robert Wecker, Tremayne Cryer

6.
Client　　　*Queen of Sheba Restaurant*
Designers　 Karen Wippich, Jon Wippich

7.
Client　　　*Bold Lions Creative*
　　　　　　Arts Education
Designers　 Robert Wecker, Tremayne Cryer

8.
Client　　　*Bonneville Environmental*
　　　　　　Foundation
Designers　 Jon Wippich, Karen Wippich

9.
Client　　　*Rulespace*
Designers　 Jon Wippich, Karen Wippich

10.
Client　　　*South Shore*
Designer　　Craig Fuller
Illustrator　Tracy Sabin

11.
Client　　　*Berkeley Farms*
Designer　　Tim McGrath
Illustrator　Tracy Sabin

12.
Client　　　*Canyon Hills*
Designers　 Craig Fuller, Sandra Sharp

13.
Client　　　*SeaCountry Homes*
Designers　 Craig Fuller, Sandra Sharp
Illustrator　Tracy Sabin

14.
Client　　　*Ken LeGros Photography*
Designers　 Jon Wippich, Karen Wippich

15.
Client　　　*Douglas Wilson Compainies*
Designers　 Sandra Sharp, Craig Fuller
Illustrator　Tracy Sabin

1.

2.

3.

4.

5.

6.

7.

1.

2.

3.

4.

5.

6.

7.

8.

9.

10.

COMPUTER DATA SOURCE

11.

12.

13.

14.

15.

1, 5, 7, 9, 10, 12, 14			8.		
Design Firm **Sabingrafik, Inc.**				Client	*Catalyst Consulting Services*
2 - 4, 6,				Designer	Kanako Yamamoto
Design Firm **The Wecker Group**			9.		
8, 11, 13, 15				Client	*Brookfield Homes*
Design Firm **Miravo Communications**				Designer	Craig Fuller
1.				Illustrator	Tracy Sabin
	Client	*Gator by the Bay*	10.		
	Designer	Thom Podgoretsky		Client	*Sabingrafik, Inc.*
	Illustrator	Tracy Sabin		Designer	Tracy Sabin
2.			11.		
	Client	*The Pebble Beach Company*		Client	*CDS*
	Designer	Robert Wecker		Designer	Steve Yasin
3.			12.		
	Client	*Fasback*		Client	*Seafarer Baking Co.*
	Designers	Robert Wecker, Tremayne Cryer		Designer	Tracy Sabin
4.			13.		
	Client	*Gainey Suites Hotel*		Client	*Kona Kofé*
	Designer	Robert Wecker		Designer	Jerry Lustan
5.			14.		
	Client	*Sabingrafik, Inc.*		Client	*Greens.com*
	Designer	Tracy Sabin		Designer	Dann Wilson
6.				Illustrator	Tracy Sabin
	Client	*Access Monterey Peninsula*	15.		
	Designer	Robert Wecker		Client	*exstream*
7.				Designer	Reece Quinones
	Client	*Brookfield Homes*			
	Designer	Craig Fuller			
	Illustrator	Tracy Sabin			

Textile Museum of Canada

1.

SECTION|EIGHT

2.

HEALTHWINDS
THE HEALTH AND WELLNESS SPA

3.

azonic
NETWORKS

4.

011LUCID11

5.

industry.

6.

7.

atmosphere

8.

108

Global Fluency

9.

Break the Cycle

Empowering Youth to End
Domestic Violence

10.

youdai

11.

STUDIO 1/6

12.

senscom

*Your Wireless Window
To The Financial World*

13.

CAMPION WALKER

garden design

❖

15.

JOHNFRIEDMANALICEKIMMARCHITECTS

14.

1.

2.

3.

4.

5.

6.

7.

8.

9.

INTERFACE

10.

11.

RENO
▶ **TECHNOLOGY** ◀

12.

13.

sm

VĪZWORX

14. **VISUALSOLUTIONS**

15.

1.

2.

3.

4.

5.

6.

7.

8.

9.

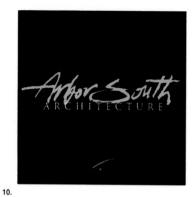

10.

Tanja Hausner

Kostümdesigns

11.

12.

Mühlbauer

13.

FRIENDS

OF LOS GATOS PUBLIC LIBRARY

15.

1, 2, 6
  Design Firm **Z•D Studios**
3 - 5, 7
  Design Firm **DotZero Design**
8
  Design Firm **Davies Associates**
9
  Design Firm **Desbrow & Associates**
10
  Design Firm **Funk & Associates**
11 - 14
  Design Firm **motterdesign, Siegmund Motter**
15
  Design Firm **Patt Mann Berry Design**
1.
  Client   *Green Bay Packers*
  Designers   Tina Remy, Mark Schmitz
2.
  Client   *Polar Sports*
  Designers   Tina Remy, Mark Schmitz
3.
  Client   *Thinkstream*
  Designers   Jon Wippich, Karen Wippich
4.
  Client   *Anita Whitesel*
  Designers   Karen Wippich, Jon Wippich
5.
  Client   *Digital Planet*
  Designers   Jon Wippich, Karen Wippich

6.
  Client   *Green Bay Packers*
  Designers   Tina Remy, Mark Schmitz
7.
  Client   *Photo 2000*
  Designers   Karen Wippich, Jon Wippich
8.
  Client   *Bedford Outpatient
              Surgery Center*
  Designers   Cathy Davies, Drew Padrutt
9.
  Client   *Vocollect—Talkman*
  Designers   Susan Rupert, Brian Lee Campbell
10.
  Client   *Arbor South Architecture*
  Designer   Chris Berner
11.
  Client   *Mrs. Tanja Hausner*
  Designer   Siegmund Motter
12.
  Client   *DAVID-optics*
  Designer   Siegmund Motter
13.
  Client   *Mühlbauer*
  Designer   Siegmund Motter
14.
  Client   *e-fundresearch.com*
  Designer   Siegmund Motter
15.
  Client   *Friends of Los Gatos Public Library*
  Designer   Patt Mann-Berry

DATABASICS
Stay Ahead

1.

MIRAVO
COMMUNICATIONS

2.

Country
Home
Mortgage

Home Finance Division of Valley Farm Credit

3.

SUPRTEK

4.

INTERSECT™
SOFTWARE

5.

VALORSYSTEMS

6.

ActiveInnovations

7.

TrustCheck®

8.

CORBETT
TECHNOLOGIES

9.

BUSINESS
APPRECIATION WEEK

Saluting those who make Virginia work

10.

alogent
Converging Payments

11.

WAYSIDE
T H E A T R E
——— Celebrating 40 years ———

12.

CHINATOWN
restaurant

13.

Knowledge Based Systems

14.

Terra
Cotta

K I T C H E N

15.

1, 2, 4 - 9, 11, 14
Design Firm **Miravo Communications**
3, 10, 12, 13, 15
Design Firm **Power/Warner**
Communications Group

1.
Client   *Databasics*
Designer   Kanako Yamamoto
2.
Client   *Miravo Communications*
Designer   Jerry Lustan
3.
Client   *Valley Farm Credit*
Designer   Mark Poole
4.
Client   *Suprtek*
Designer   Steve Yasin
5.
Client   *Intersect Software*
Designer   Kanako Yamamoto
6.
Client   *Valor Systems*
Designer   Kanako Yamamoto
7.
Client   *info Router*
Designer   Kanako Yamamoto

8.
Client   *Global Integrity*
Designer   Steve Yasin
9.
Client   *Corbett Technologies*
Designer   Kanako Yamamoto
10.
Client   *Virginia Department of Business Assistance*
Designer   Sharon Snyder
11.
Client   *Alogent*
Designer   Jerry Lustan
12.
Client   *Wayside Theatre*
Designer   Mark Poole
13.
Client   *Chinatown Restaurant*
Designer   Josie Fertig
14.
Client   *Knowledge-Based Systems*
Designer   Kanako Yamamoto
15.
Client   *Terra Cotta Kitchen*
Designer   Mark Poole

1.

2.

3.

4.

Alcott Routon

Direct. Results.

5.

6.

7.

1 - 3, 6
Design Firm **Tribe Design, Inc.**
4, 5, 7
Design Firm **VNO**
1.
  Client   *Third Arm Solutions*
  Designers Francisco Rios, Aramis Nunez
2.
  Client   *Council for Environmental Education*
  Designers Francisco Rios, Patrick Racelis
3.
  Client   *Diagnostic Marketing Group*
  Designers Kristen Rubin, Aramis Nunez
4.
  Client   *Ryman Auditorium*
  Designer Jim Vienneau
5.
  Client   *Alcott Routon*
  Designer Jim Vienneau

6.
  Client   *Houston Used Car Network*
  Designers Francisco Rios, Aramis Nunez
7.
  Client   *Tembo*
  Designer Jim Vienneau
opposite
Design Firm **Capstone Studios Inc.**
  Client   *Hilly Pitzer/People Magazine*
  Designers John Taylor Dismukes,
              JoAnne Redwood

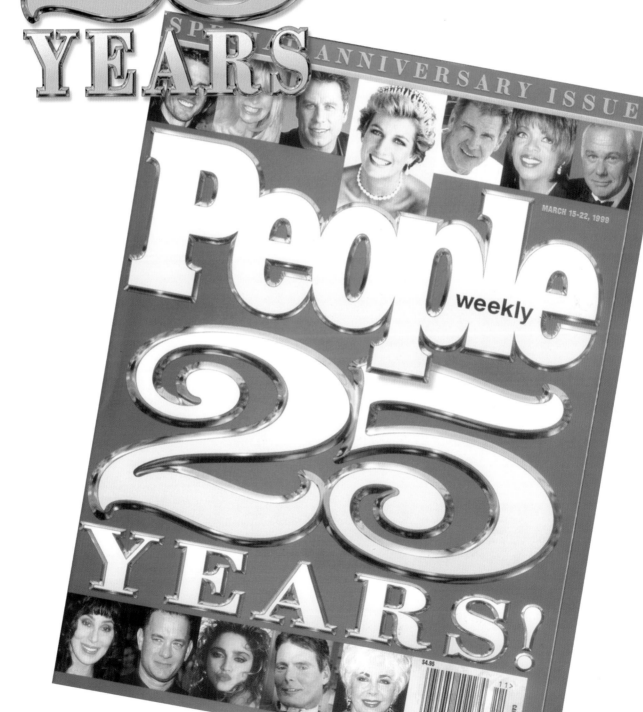

1.

2.

BETHEL
CONSTRUCTION

3.

4.

PINCKNEY
PHOTOGRAPHY

5.

6.

7.

8.

hullaballoo
bold american cooking

9.

10.

Properties, Inc.

11.

12.

13.

14.

A Journey Through Our Solar System

15.

1 - 13		
Design Firm	**The Wecker Group**	
14, 15		
Design Firm	**Groff Creative, Inc.**	
1.		
Client	*Couture Events*	
Designer	Robert Wecker	
2.		
Client	*Traveleze.com*	
Designer	Robert Wecker	
3.		
Client	*Bethel Construction*	
Designers	Robert Wecker, Tremayne Cryer	
4.		
Client	*Carmel by the Sea.com*	
Designer	Robert Wecker	
5.		
Client	*Pinckney Photography*	
Designer	Robert Wecker	
6.		
Client	*Inns of California*	
Designer	Robert Wecker	
7.		
Client	*River Ranch Vineyards*	
Designer	Robert Wecker	

8.	
Client	*Monterey Cowboy Poetry & Music Festival*
Designer	Robert Wecker
9.	
Client	*Hullaballoo*
Designer	Robert Wecker
10.	
Client	*Wendy Dean Productions*
Designer	Robert Wecker
11.	
Client	*Di Nuovo Properties, Inc.*
Designer	Robert Wecker
12.	
Client	*City of Monterey, Ca.*
Designer	Robert Wecker
13.	
Client	*Monterey Country Inn*
Designer	Robert Wecker
14.	
Client	*Centennial of Flight Commission*
Designer	Jay Groff
15.	
Client	*Smithsonian Institution Traveling Exhibit Service, Challenger Center for Space Science Education and National Aeronautics and Space Administration*
Designer	Jay Groff

1.

2.

3.

4.

5.

6.

7.

8.

9.

*the***edsite**.com

10.

11.

EST. 1999

GREATLODGE

12.

élan

13.

SimplyShe

14.

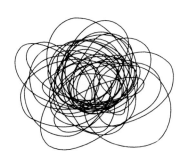

new**energy**

15.

1.

2.

3.

4.

5.

6.

7.

8.

9.

10.

11.

12.

TOWNHALLAMERICA.com

13.

14.

15.

1 - 3, 5, 9, 10, 12 - 14
Design Firm **MFDI**
4, 6 - 8, 11, 15
Design Firm **Gardner Design**

1.
Client — *Kingswood-Oxford School*
Designers — Rich Hilliard, Mark Fertig

2, 3
Client — *Encore*
Designers — Mark Fertig, Jon Walker

4.
Client — *Artistree*
Designer — Brian Miller

5.
Client — *Transtec*
Designer — Mark Fertig

6.
Client — *Power Reach*
Designer — Brian Miller

7.
Client — *Amber Lear*
Designer — Brian Miller

8.
Client — *Wichitas Promise*
Designer — Brian Miller

9.
Client — *The Golf Man*
Designer — Mark Fertig

10.
Client — *Mid-Pax*
Designers — Sarah Marcis, Mark Fertig

11.
Client — *CSRD*
Designer — Bill Gardner

12.
Client — *MFDI*
Designers — Rich Hilliard, Mark Fertig

13.
Client — *Graham Partners*
Designers — Rich Hilliard, Mark Fertig

14.
Client — *MFDI*
Designer — Mark Fertig

15.
Client — *Gardner Design*
Designer — Bill Gardner

1. PARKWAYS

FOUNDATION

PRIVATE FUNDING FOR PUBLIC GREATNESS

2.

3.

4.

5. WYOMING BOOK™

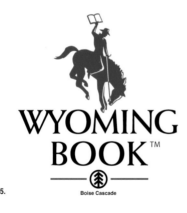

Boise Cascade

6.

7.

8.

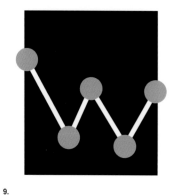

9.

Cater First

10.

EFFERVÉ®
SPARKLING

11.

12.

13.

Fannie Mae
TECH PAK

14.

miami
children's
museum

15.

1, 4, 5
Design Firm **Davis Harrison Dion**
2
Design Firm **Dever Designs**
3, 6
Design Firm **DGWB**
7
Design Firm **Cipriano Advertising**
8
Design Firm **Addison**
9
Design Firm **LekasMiller Design**
10, 13
Design Firm **Levine & Associates**
11, 15
Design Firm **Selbert Perkins Design**
12
Design Firm **H2D**
14
Design Firm **Graves Fowler Associates**

1.
Client *Parkways Foundation*
Designers Phil Schuldt, Bob Dion
2.
Client *Climate Institute*
Designer Jeffrey L. Dever
3.
Client *Toshiba EID*
Designers Jonathan Brown, Swen Igawa
4.
Client *Chicago Convention & Tourism Bureau*
Designer Bob Dion

5.
Client *Boise Cascade*
Designers Brent Vincent, Phil Schuldt
6.
Client *JAX*
Designers Jonathan Brown, Sven Igawa
7.
Client *Turnberry Place*
Designer Rick Cooper
8.
Client *Intelsat*
Designers David Kohler, Nicolas Zentner
9.
Client *Weinsheimer Group*
Designer Lana Ip
10.
Client *Cater First*
Designer Monica Snellings
11.
Client *Eurobubblies*
Designers Robin Perkins, Georgia Robrecht
12.
Client *H2D*
Designers Joseph Hausch, Allan Haas, Terry Lutz
13.
Designer Lena Markley
14.
Client *Fannie Mae*
Designer Victoria Q. Robinson
15.
Client *Miami Children's Museum*
Designers C. Selbert, K. Burke, S. Bates, J. Kitmitto, J. Lutz

1.

2.

3.

4.

5.

6.

7.

8.

9.

10.

11.

12.

13.

BOX.COM

14.

15.

1 - 15		
Design Firm **MFDI**		

1.
Client — *Bird Play*
Designers — Rich Hilliard, Mark Fertig

2.
Client — *Comptrends, USA*
Designer — Mark Fertig

3.
Client — *Internet Sheet.com*
Designer — Mark Fertig

4.
Client — *eBone*
Designer — Mark Fertig

5.
Client — *Labels-R-Us*
Designers — Kevin Pitts, Mark Fertig

6.
Client — *Jaco Industrials*
Designer — Mark Fertig

7.
Client — *True Logic*
Designer — Mark Fertig

8.
Client — *Giftline*
Designer — Mark Fertig

9.
Client — *Paint Jockeys*
Designer — Mark Fertig

10.
Client — *MFDI*
Designers — Trudy Ha, Mark Fertig

11.
Client — *Opportunity.com*
Designer — Mark Fertig

12.
Client — *Tiger Brands*
Designer — Mark Fertig

13.
Client — *Web Traffic.com*
Designer — Mark Fertig

14.
Client — *Box.com*
Designer — Mark Fertig

15.
Client — *4 Fun Travel Agency*
Designer — Mark Fertig

1.

2.

3.

4.

5.

6.

7.

8.

9.

10.

11.

12.

14.

13.

15.

1, 3		**7.**	
Design Firm	**Ray Braun Graphic Design**	Client	*Incipience*
2, 4 - 7		Designers	Rich Hilliard, Mark Fertig
Design Firm	**MFDI**	**8.**	
8		Client	*Clark Retail Enterprises:*
Design Firm	**Addison**		*Oh! Zone*
9, 12, 13		Designers	Kraig Kessel, Matt Versue,
Design Firm	**Robert Meyers Design**		Nick Bently
10, 11		**9.**	
Design Firm	**Wet Paper Bag**	Client	*Articulate Inc.*
	Visual Communication	Designer	Robert Meyers
14, 15		**10.**	
Design Firm	**Design Center**	Client	*TCU Visual Communication*
1.			*Program*
Client	*Berean Bible Church*	Designer	Lewis Glaser
Designer	Ray Braun	**11.**	
2.		Client	*National Dance Association*
Client	*Solid Crystal*	Designer	Lewis Glaser
Designer	Mark Fertig	**12.**	
3.		Client	*Articulate Inc.*
Client	*German Retirement Home*	Designer	Robert Meyers
Designer	Ray Braun	**13.**	
4.		Client	*Articulate Inc.*
Client	*eloise rae*	Designer	Robert Meyers
Designer	Mark Fertig	**14.**	
5.		Client	*Taraccino Coffee*
Client	*xSalvage.com*	Designers	John Reger, Todd Spichke
Designers	Kevin Pitts, Mark Fertig	**15.**	
6.		Client	*State of Minnesota*
Client	*Athletic Education Resources*	Designers	John Reger, Dan Olson
Designer	Mark Fertig		

1.

2.

3.

4.

5.

6.

7.

8.

CHRISTMAS
CAROL

9.

10.

KIDS.NET

11.

Big River

THE ADVENTURES
OF HUCKLEBERRY FINN

12.

eMarineOnline.com

SUPPLY CHAIN SOLUTIONS

13.

14.

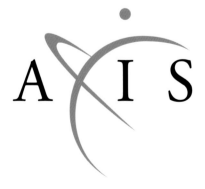

AXIS

15.

1.

UNIVERSITY INN
AND CONFERENCE CENTER
AT RUTGERS

2.

World Tours

3.

ipro

4.

**ACTORS THEATER
OF MINNESOTA**

5.

GOTHAM

6.

OPINN SKÓGUR

7.

fried Bananas
CUBAN FOOD

8.

9.

11.

13.

15.

Flonase®

10.

Princeton
Leadership
Consulting, L.L.C.
Your Catalyst for Business Solutions

12.

HAGE FINANCIAL SERVICES INC.
INNOVATIVE FINANCING SOLUTIONS FOR BUSINESS.

14.

1.

2.

3.

4.

5. EE**Z**EE
COMB & STYLE

6. *Arlington* *Million*
Room

7.

8.

134

R2wow.com

9.

OneSpiritOneWorld Inc.

10.

heartrings

11.

THE
LINE DRIVE
★ Est. 2001

12.

AVIATOR'S grill

13.

the
Flight deck

14.

THE
HITCHING POST

15.

FRJÁLSI
FJÁRFESTINGARBANKINN

1.

FAIRFAX
C O R N E R

2.

3.

MUSEUMS & SPECIAL EVENTS

4.

THREE RIVERS RAMBLER

5.

6.

7.

8.

INDIANA QUADEL

INDIANA **QUADEL**

9.

TENNESSEE **QUADEL**

10.

James Buchanan

F O U N D A T I O N

For the Preservation of Wheatland
Home of the 15th President of the United States

11.

12.

T·I·L·E·O·L·O·G·Y

THE STUDY OF COMFORT AND STYLE

14.

The Orthopædic Group

13.

15.

1
Design Firm **Gott Folk McCann-Erickson**
2
Design Firm **Development Design Group, Inc.**
3, 7
Design Firm **EDAW, Inc.**
4
Design Firm **Inc 3**
5, 6
Design Firm **Richard Design Group**
8
Design Firm **Hornall Anderson Design Works**
9
Design Firm **Pensaré Design Group**
10, 13, 15
Design Firm **Dyad Communications, Inc.**
11, 12, 14
Design Firm **Dean Design/**
Marketing Group, Inc.

1.
Client   *Frjâlsi Investment Bank*
Designer   Hjörvar Hardarson
2.
Client   *Steiner + Associates*
Designer   Amanda Moreau
3.
Client   *EDAW, Inc.*
Designer   Marty McGraw
4.
Client   *Muse*
Designers   Harvey Appelbaum,
                Christopher Nystrom
5.
Client   *Three Rivers Rambler*
Designers   Tommy Stokes, Michael Richards

6.
Client   *Cheetah Recreational Equipment*
Designers   Timothy Jenkins, Michael Richards
7.
Client   *EDAW, Inc.*
Designer   Marty McGraw
8.
Client   *Big Island Candies*
Designers   Jack Anderson, Kathy Saito, Mary
                Chin Hutchison, Alan Copeland
9.
Client   *Quadel Consulting Corporation*
Designer   Kundia D. Wood
10.
Client   *Institute for the Study of*
                Conflict Transformation
Designer   Tom Maciag
11.
Client   *James Buchanan Foundation*
Designer   Jeff Phillips
12.
Client   *Prudhomme's Lost Cajun Kitchen*
Designer   Lori Hess
13.
Client   *The Orthopaedic Group*
Designer   Tom Maciag
14.
Client   *Tileology*
Designer   Jeff Phillips
15.
Client   *The Institute of*
                Classical Architecture
Designer   Tom Maciag

1.

2.

3.

4.

5.

6.

7.

8.

9.

P R I S M
Color Corporation

10.

*Confidence**Plus*™

11.

Strategic
Alliances

12.

interactived4

13.

B⊠X
O F F I C E

14.

15.

1.

2.

3.

Discovery Technology Center
Cambridge, Massachusetts

4.

Montessori
Children's House of Valley Forge

5.

6.

7.

8.

9.

10.

11.

STRATEGIC
WORKFORCE SOLUTIONS

12.

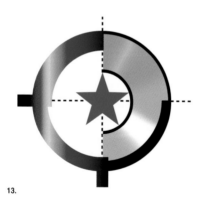

13.

MISSION: 47TH ANNUAL CONFERENCE
POSSIBLE KAB

14.

15.

1. **Corning**Orientation

mi|casa

2.

SAFARI TRAVEL
P L A N N E R S

3.

MEDIA S O L U T I O N S

4.

SPORTS AFIELD
TEXAS
SPORTSMAN'S
F A I R

5.

ARTSfest

6.

the
Spa

7.

PELOSI CHAMBERS
PHOTOGRAPHY

8.

9.

a festival of art

10.

BIJAN
INTERNATIONAL

11.

12.

neon

14.

13.

15.

1.

2.

3.

4.

5.

6.

7.

8.

designRoomcreative

9.

10.

11.

Pet Express

12.

RYAN + ASSOCIATES

13.

NEOSA

14.

USPC

15.

1.

2.

3.

4.

5.

6.

7.

8.

9.

10.

ROSE RECYCLING
A WOMAN OWNED ENTERPRISE

11.

12.

13.

14.

15.

1.

2.

3.

4.

5.

6.

7.

8.

9.

10.

11.

12.

13.

14.

15.

1 - 15
Design Firm **MFDI**

1.
Client   *Show Me Tickets*
Designer   Mark Fertig

2.
Client   *Computer Environments*
Designer   Mark Fertig

3.
Client   *Flywheel Ventures*
Designer   Mark Fertig

4.
Client   *Planters Direct*
Designer   Mark Fertig

5.
Client   *1 Cork St.*
Designers   Mike Barkley, Mark Fertig

6.
Client   *Cookbook Creations*
Designers   Rich Hilliard, Mark Fertig

7.
Client   *How Ya Bean?*
Designers   Mike Barkley, Mark Fertig

8.
Client   *Golden Wonder*
Designer   Mark Fertig

9.
Client   *Grassy Hill*
Designer   Mark Fertig

10.
Client   *Debate Coach*
Designers   Kevin Pitts, Mark Fertig

11.
Client   *Rose Murex*
Designer   Mark Fertig

12.
Client   *Arcade Bandits*
Designer   Mark Fertig

13.
Client   *The Eccentric Gardener*
Designer   Mark Fertig

14.
Client   *eWorkingWomen.com*
Designers   Lindsay Ebersole, Mark Fertig

15.
Client   *Biltmore Homes*
Designer   Mark Fertig

1.

extremetix

2.

PARK
School
TUDOR
Hall
100
YEARS OF EXCELLENCE

3.

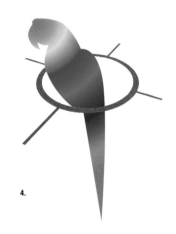

4.

AIDS Community Resources

5.

Community
&
Family
Resource Center

6.

LEADERSHIP
GREATER SYRACUSE

7.

8.   Foxton Farm

150

9.

10.

11.

12.

13.

Layer2 Networks℠

14.

15.

151

1.

2. OLYMPIC
MEDICAL CENTER

3. NORTHAMERICAN
BANK

4.

5. MULTIMEDIA

6. NORTHSTAR

7. MADRONA
Philanthropy Services

8.

9.

Taking The Initiative

10.

Patera

11.

BRAZIL

on the HILL

12.

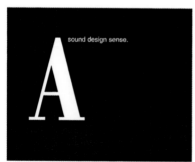

A sound design sense.

13.

CITYNET℠

14.

FINGER LAKES WINE COUNTRY

VISITOR

C E N T E R

1.

2.

3.

4.

5.

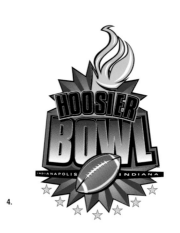

6.

7.

8.

9.

10.

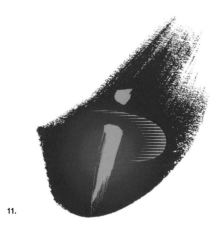

11.

INDIANA
STATE MUSEUM

12.

CREST

13.

PEOPLE DEELOPER
SINGAPORE

14.

CAREGIVER

15.

1.

COALITION FOR
Women's Basketball

2.

3.

4.

GOOD
SAMARITAN
CENTER
of the Episcopal Diocese of West Texas

5.

6.

7.

8.

9.

10.

11.

12.

ARTEXT   ARTEXT

ARTEXT   ARTEXT

13.

SART_M

14.

POPE JOHN PAUL II
• CULTURAL CENTER •

15.

157

1.

2.

3.

4.

5.

6.

7.

8.

9.

10.

11.

12.

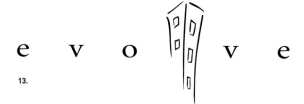

13.

14.

15.

1.

2.

LASERPACIFIC

MEDIA CORPORATION

3.

KINZAN

4.

5.

6.

von Gal Associates

7.

8.

KENNYBROWN

The Fusion of Performance, Engineering and Style

9.

10.

N E T I S U N ™

11.

stēl OBJEKT

F u r n i t u r e   f o r   t h e   S o u l

12.

13.

14.

OPTIONS
BY DESIGN
INCORPORATED

15.

1, 2, 5, 6,
Design Firm **Sayles Graphic Design**
3, 4, 7
Design Firm **Visual Asylum**
8, 9, 11, 12, 14
Design Firm **Planet 10**
10
Design Firm **Wilmer Fong + Associates**
13
Design Firm **Design North**
15
Design Firm **Options By Design**

1.
   Client   *Jordan Motors*
   Designer   John Sayles
2.
   Client   *Iowa Metal Fabrication*
   Designer   John Sayles
3.
   Client   *Laser Pacific*
   Designer   Joel Sotelo
4.
   Client   *Kinzan*
   Designer   Joel Sotelo
5.
   Client   *Sayles Graphic Design
               "Biker Boy"*
   Designer   John Sayles

6.
   Client   *Waterbury Neighborhood
               Association*
   Designer   John Sayles
7.
   Client   *Von Gal Associates*
   Designer   Amy Jo Levine
8.
   Client   *Indianapolis Motor Speedway*
   Designer   Mike Tuttle
9.
   Client   *Kenny Brown*
   Designers   Mike Tuttle, Jennifer Tuttle
10.
   Client   *The Clorox Company*
   Designer   Tim Ferdun
11.
   Client   *Netisun*
   Designer   Mike Tuttle
12.
   Client   *Stel Objekt*
   Designer   Mike Tuttle
13.
   Client   *4 Seasons Car Wash*
   Designer   Volker Beckmann
14.
   Client   *Clarian Health*
   Designer   Jennifer Tuttle
15.
   Client   *Options By Design*
   Designers   Jeff Wright, Marie Corfield

1.

2.

3.

4.

5.

6.

7.

8.

9.

10.

11.

12.

13.

14.

15.

1 - 4, 6, 9 - 13
Design Firm **Visual Asylum**
5, 14
Design Firm **Sabingrafik, Inc.**
7, 8, 15
Design Firm **Planet 10**

1.
Client   *The Reserve*
Designer   Joel Sotelo
2.
Client   *The Reserve*
Designer   Joel Sotelo
3.
Client   *Congo Jacks*
Designer   Amy Jo Levine
4.
Client   *The Reserve*
Designer   Joel Sotelo
5.
Client   *AIRS*
Designers   James Schenck,
              David Forman
Illustrator   Tracy Sabin

6.
Client   *2 to Tango*
Designer   Joel Sotelo
7.
Client   *Radius*
Designer   Mike Tuttle
8.
Client   *Escient Convergence*
Designer   Mike Tuttle
9 - 11.
Client   *The Reserve*
Designer   Joel Sotelo
12.
Client   *Lido Peninsula*
Designer   Amy Jo Levine
13.
Client   *La Papaya*
Designer   Joel Sotelo
14.
Client   *Tamansari Beverage*
Designers   Karim Amirgani, Tracy Sabin
15.
Client   *INITA*
Designers   Jennifer Tuttle, Tina Smith

1.

2.

3.

4.

5.

6.

7.

8.

9.

10.

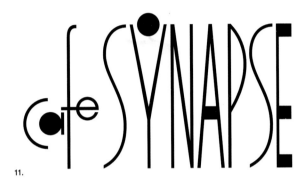

11.

12.

Landscape Development

14.

(Borsani) } **Comunicazione**

13.

15.

1.

SPIDER SECURITIES

2.

3.

4.

5.

6.

7.

PARC METROPOLITAN

8.

166

9.

10.

11.

12.

13.

visual  asylum

14.

15.

1, 7
   Design Firm **Sabingrafik, Inc.**
2 - 5, 8, 12, 14
   Design Firm **Visual Asylum**
6, 11, 15
   Design Firm **Sayles Graphic Design**
9
   Design Firm **Pirman Communications Inc.**
10
   Design Firm **J.J. Sedelmaier Prod., Inc.**
13
   Design Firm **Big Bang Idea Engineering**
1.
   Client   *Sabingrafik, Inc.*
   Designer   Tracy Sabin
2.
   Client   *Spiders Securities*
   Designer   Charles Glaubitz
3 - 5.
   Client   *Bottleneck Blues Bar*
   Designer   Joel Sotelo
6.
   Client   *Hotel Fort Des Moines*
   Designer   John Sayles
7.
   Client   *Taylor Guitars*
   Designers   Rita Hoffman, Tracy Sabin

8.
   Client   *Parc Metropolitan*
   Designer   Joel Sotelo
9.
   Client   *Long Family*
   Designer   Brian Pirman
10.
   Client   *NBC/Saturday Night Live*
   Designer   J.J. Sedelmaier
11.
   Client   *Jimmy's American Cafe*
   Designer   John Sayles
12.
   Client   *Ghemm*
   Designer   Joel Sotelo
13.
   Client   *San Diego Advertising Fund
               for Emergencies*
   Designer   Myles McGuinness
   Illustrator Tracy Sabin
14.
   Client   *Visual Asylum*
   Designers   Joel Sotelo, Lizette Picazo
15.
   Client   *Pattee Enterprises
               (2000 Arts & Crafts conference)*
   Designer   John Sayles

1.

2.

WIRED
environments

3.

4.

5.

6.

7.

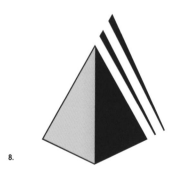

8.

9.

10.

11.

12.

13.

College of St. Joseph

14.

15.

1 - 3, 5 - 9, 11, 13, 15
Design Firm **Mike Quon/Designation**
4
Design Firm **RTKL Associates Inc./ID8**
10, 12, 14
Design Firm **Set?Communicate!**

1.
| Client | *phone vision* |
| Designer | Mike Quon |

2.
| Client | *Wired Environments* |
| Designers | Mike Quon, Anna Moreira |

3.
| Client | *AT+T* |
| Designers | Mike Quon, Anna Moreira |

4.
| Client | *Old Mutual Properties* |
| Designers | Greg Rose, Young Choe, Thom McKay |

5.
| Client | *Woody Allen* |
| Designers | Mike Quon, Anna Moreira |

6.
| Client | *Eastern Environmental* |
| Designer | Mike Quon |

7.
| Client | *Reuters* |
| Designer | Mike Quon |

8.
| Client | *Unilogic* |
| Designers | Mike Quon, Anna Moreira |

9.
| Client | *New York Life* |
| Designer | Mike Quon |

10.
| Client | *Church of the Beloved* |
| Designers | Steve Thomas, Dan Wold |

11.
| Client | *Unity Technology* |
| Designers | Mike Quon, Anna Moreira |

12.
| Client | *Omega Global* |
| Designers | Steve Thomas, Dan Wold |

13.
| Client | *The National Conference* |
| Designer | Mike Quon |

14.
| Client | *College of St. Joseph* |
| Designers | Steve Thomas, Dan Wold |

15.
| Client | *KPMG Consulting* |
| Designers | Mike Quon, Anna Moreira |

1.

2.

3.

4.

5.

6.

7.

8.

170

Authentic. Diverse. CALIFORNIA.

9.

AGE CONCERNS

10.

BIO DIVERSITY

11.

Ertl Collectibles

12.

Snap-on

13.

LMP|NYC

14.

15.

1.

2.

3.

COLLEGE PLACE NUTRITION
Smoothie Supreme

4.

5.

6.

7.

8.

9.

10.

11.

LES ALIMENTS FINS
LE DUC

12.

P L Y W O O D   T A C O M A ,   I N C .

13.

ÉCRITS DES HAUTES~TERRES

14.

15.

1
Design Firm **EAT Advertising and Design**
2, 3, 5, 8, 11, 12, 14, 15
Design Firm **Iridium, a design agency**
4, 6, 7, 9, 13
Design Firm **Creo Design**
10
Design Firm **Mike Quon/Designation**

1.
Client   *Sunflower Broadband*
Designers   Patrice Eilts-Jobe,
            Jeremy Shellhorn
2.
Client   *Magpie Communications*
Designer   Jean-Luc Denat
3.
Client   *Co-Creations*
Designer   Mario L'Écuyer
4.
Client   *College Place Nutrition*
Designer   Colin Magnuson
5.
Client   *PowerTrunk*
Designer   Mario L'Écuyer
6.
Client   *DuPont Dental*
Designer   Colin Magnuson

7.
Client   *LoanTek*
Designer   Colin Magnuson
8.
Client   *Nygem*
Designers   Mario L'Écuyer,
            Jean-Luc Denat
9.
Client   *Sunshine Metals*
Designer   Colin Magnuson
10.
Client   *Muze (Metro Media)*
Designer   Mike Quon
11.
Client   *CRC (Canadian Research Chairs)*
Designer   Mario L'Écuyer
12.
Client   *Les aliments fins Le Duc*
Designer   Jean-Luc Denat
13.
Client   *Plytac*
Designer   Colin Magnuson
14.
Client   *Écrits des Hautes-Terres*
Designers   Jean-Luc Denat, Etienne Bessette
15.
Client   *CPRN (Canadian Policy
            Research Networks)*
Designer   Mario L'Écuyer

173

1.

MIKIMOTO

2.

Dch*

3. **the**Documentary**channel**

Baas & Associates PC
growing your business

4.

Willard
ON THE TOWN
catering

5.

genesis

6.

grille

7.

cultura~

8.

174

PUERTO RICO
CONVENTION CENTER
at the Americas World Trade District

9.

10.

11.

12.

13.

14.

15.

1, 4
  Design Firm **Dotzler Creative Arts**
2, 3, 8, 15
  Design Firm **Arnell Group**
5, 7, 9, 12, 13,
  Design Firm **The Campbell Group**
6, 10, 11, 14
  Design Firm **Melia Design Group**
1.
  Client   *Trinity Interdenominational Church*
2.
  Client   *Mikimoto*
  Designer   Peter Arnell
3.
  Client   *The Documentary Channel*
  Designers Peter Arnell, Mike Doyle
4.
  Client   *Baas & Associates*
5.
  Client   *The Willard Inter-Continental Hotel*
  Designer   Joanne Westerman
6.
  Client   *Genesis*
  Designer   Frank Chen

7.
  Client   *The Baltimore Marriott
             Waterfront Hotel*
  Designer   Joanne Westerman
8.
  Client   *Cultura*
  Designer   Peter Arnell
9.
  Client   *The Puerto Rico
             Convention Center*
  Designer   Joanne Westerman
10.
  Client   *Return.com*
  Designer   Frank Chen
11.
  Client   *EZ Fizz (Coca-Cola)*
  Designers Shai Harris, Frank Chen
12.
  Client   *The Baltimore Marriott
             Waterfront Hotel*
  Designer   Joanne Westerman
13.
  Client   *The Willard Inter-Continental Hotel*
  Designer   Joanne Westerman
14.
  Client   *Intercontinental Exchange*
  Designer   Jeff Brostoff
15.
  Client   *Pass Entertainment*
  Designers Peter Arnell, Mike Doyle

H.O.P.E.

Highmark Osteoporosis Prevention and Education Program

1.

LIDIA VARESCO

2. DESIGN

Pinnacle

AT BRICKYARD LANDING

3.

4.

RIVERMARK

o f   S a n t a   C l a r a

5.

HIGHGROVE
AT DUBLIN RANCH

6.

7.

OUTLOOK HEIGHTS

8.

9.

11.

CULINARY REVOLUTION

13.

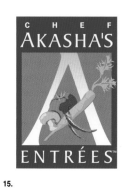

15.

Ozark Homes and Property.com

10.

OzarkHealth.com

12.

OzarkDoctors.com

14.

1.

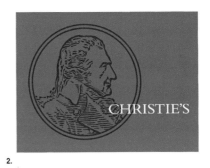

2.

3.

4.

5.

6.

7.

8.

Se·man·tix

9.

10.

HONDA RACING

11.

THE GIVING TREE

12.

Valley Lahvosh Baking Co.
THE BAKERY WITH A HEART · SINCE 1922

13.

ENSPHERICS

14.

15.

1, 8, 10
   Design Firm **Pandora and Company**
2
   Design Firm **Carbone Smolan Agency**
3 - 5, 7, 9, 11, 12, 14, 15
   Design Firm **Evenson Design Group**
6
   Design Firm **Dart Design**
13
   Design Firm **Janice Barrett Design**
1.
   Client   *San Luis Obispo County Parks Dept.*
   Designers Stephanie Fernandez, Pandora Nash-Karner
2.
   Client   *Christie's*
   Designers Claire Taylor, Sharon Slaughter Koi Vantanapahu
3.
   Client   *Acura Music Festival*
   Designers Stan Evenson, Glenn Sakamoto, Jill Maida
4.
   Client   *Angel City Fitness*
   Designers Stan Evenson, Mark Sojka
5.
   Client   *St. Vincent Medical Center*
   Designers Stan Evenson, Judy K. Lee, John Krause
6.
   Client   *Great River Golf Club*
   Designers David Anderson, Linda Anderson

7.
   Client   *Honda Corporation*
   Designers Stan Evenson, Mark Sojka, John Krause
8.
   Client   *San Luis Obispo County Visitor's Bureau*
   Designers Stephanie Fernandez, Pandora Nash-Karner
9.
   Client   *Semantix*
   Designer Mark Sojka
10.
   Client   *Los Osos Community Services District*
   Designers Cynthia Milhem, Paula Cavallara Pandora Nash-Karner
11.
   Client   *Honda Corporation*
   Designers Stan Evenson, Mark Sojka, John Krause
12.
   Client   *The Giving Tree*
   Designers Stan Evenson, Mark Sojka
13.
   Client   *Valley Lahuosh Baking Co.*
   Designer Janice Barrett
14.
   Client   *Enspherics*
   Designers Stan Evenson, Judy K. Lee Tricia Rauen
15.
   Client   *Idyllwild Jazz Music Festival*
   Designers Stan Evenson, Ondine Jarl

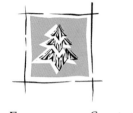

1. The Evergreen Society

2. DANCE
CLEVELAND

PARK WORKS

3.

4.

white sand villas

5.

LAND ONE

6.

7.

SCHEFFLERA SUMO

8.

180

9.

CORPORATE SYSTEMS

10.

11.

12.

13.

BREWER & TOMINAGA

14.

15.

1.

2.

3.

4.

5.

6.

7.

8.

9.

10.

11.

12.

13.

14.

15.

3.

2.

1.

7.

4.

FANTASY

5.

M E N S   POOL

6.

TeaM
Active DreaMers™

8.

9.

10.

11.

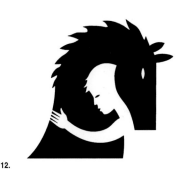

12.

13.

14.

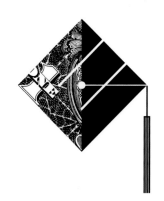

15.

1 - 4, 9 - 12
Design Firm **Greteman Group**
5, 6
Design Firm **Ukulele Design Consultants Pte Ltd**
7
Design Firm **Nichols Graphic Design**
8
Design Firm **Johnson Rauhoff Marketing**
13
Design Firm **Wet Paper Bag Visual Communication**
14, 15
Design Firm **Michael Gunselman Incorporated**

1 - 3.
Client   *Greteman Group*
Designer James Strange
4.
Client   *StepStone*
Designer Garrett Fresh
5.
Client   *Prime Electrical Products (Pte) Ltd*
Designers Kim Chun Wei, Lynn Lim
6.
Client   *Men'spool Pte Ltd*
Designers Verna Lim, Sim Choon Tee

7.
Client   *The Cooper Union*
Designer Mary Ann Nichols
8.
Client   *Judy Molnar*
Designer Mason Johnson
9.
Client   *HOK*
Designer James Strange
10.
Designer James Strange
11.
Client   *Azure Skin Care*
Designer James Strange
12.
Client   *Healing Horses Therapy*
Designers James Strange, Garrett Fresh
13.
Client   *Prometheus Publications*
Designer Lewis Glaser
14.
Client   *Foxcroft School*
Designer Michael Gunselman
15.
Client   *EduCap*
Designer Michael Gunselman

1.

2.

3.

4.

5.

6.

7.

8.

FORTERA
Technology Assurance

9.

10.

Ovation™

11.

Alkermes
Science that Delivers

12.

R|A|M

13.

pocketDBA™

14.

west

15.

1
Design Firm **Phillips Design**
2 - 5
Design Firm **Rabil & Bates Design Co.**
6
Design Firm **Gardner Design**
7 - 12
Design Firm **Addison Whitney**
13 - 15
Design Firm **Liska + Associates, Inc.**

1.
Client   *MOSI-Museum of Science &*
             Industry, Tampa, Fl.
Designer   Michael Y. Phillips

2.
Client   *Kalista Kollection*
Designer   Seth Sirbaugh

3.
Designer   Seth Sirbaugh

4.
Client   *Joelle Coretti*
Designers   Seth Sirbaugh

5.
Client   *Java Junction*
Designers   Seth Sirbaugh, Roger Selvage

6.
Client   *Loveland Properties*
Designer   Bill Gardner

7.
Client   *Genaera*
Designers   Lisa Johnston, David Honk,
            Kimberlee Davis

8.
Client   *Ascential Software*
Designers   Kimberlee Davis, Lisa Johnston
            David Honk

9.
Client   *Fortera*
Designers   David Honk, Kimberlee Davis
            Lisa Johnston

10.
Client   *Children's Miracle Network*
Designers   Lisa Johnston, David Honk,
            Kimberlee Davis

11.
Client   *VistaLab Technologies*
Designers   David Honk, Lisa Johnston
            Kimberlee Davis

12.
Client   *Alkermes*
Designers   Lisa Johnston, David Honk,
            Kimberlee Davis

13.
Client   *Racine Art Museum*
Designer   Christine Schneider

14.
Client   *PocketDBA Systems*
Designer   Steve Liska

15.
Client   *West Corporation*

1.

2.

3.

4.

5.

6.

7.

8.

9.

EmoryVision

10.

ÖSEL

11.

DELPHI
PRODUCTIONS

12.

SharpShooter Spectrum
Imaging

13.

PRIMEresponse™
Relationship marketing just got better.™

14.

15.

1, 3		
	Design Firm	**Tim Kenney Design Partners**
2, 4, 6 - 9		
	Design Firm	**Greteman Group**
5		
	Design Firm	**LPG Design**
10		
	Design Firm	**ThinkHouse Creative, Inc.**
11 - 15		
	Design Firm	**Focus Design**
1.		
	Client	*Holy Trinity Catholic Church*
	Designers	Tim Kenney, Charlene Gamba
2.		
	Client	*Flexjet*
	Designer	James Strange
3.		
	Client	*Personal Communications Industry Association*
	Designers	Tim Kenney, Monica Banko, Charlene Gamba
4.		
	Client	*Climate Works*
	Designer	James Strange
5.		
	Client	*Gourmet's Choice Roasterie*
	Designers	Lorna West, Chris West

6.		
	Client	*Executive Aircraft*
	Designer	James Strange
7.		
	Client	*Flexjet*
	Designer	James Strange
8.		
	Client	*R. Messner Construction Company*
	Designer	James Strange
9.		
	Client	*City of Wichita*
	Designer	James Strange
10.		
	Client	*Emory Vision*
	Designer	Gregg Snyder
11.		
	Client	*Osel Incorporated*
	Designer	Brian Jacobson
12.		
	Client	*Delphi Productions*
	Designer	Brian Jacobson
13.		
	Client	*Sharpshoot Spectrum*
	Designer	Brian Jacobson
14.		
	Client	*Prime Response*
	Designer	Brian Jacobson
15.		
	Client	*Appearance Salon*
	Designer	Brian Jacobson

1.

2.

3.

4.

5.

6.

7.

8.

9.

10.

11.

12.

13.

14.

15.

1
　Design Firm **Paris Design Studio**
2, 5, 8, 11 - 14
　Design Firm **Guarino Graphics**
3, 4, 6, 7, 15
　Design Firm **Focus Design**
9
　Design Firm **Nine Design**
10
　Design Firm **Simple Green**

1.
　Client　　　*Joseph Vatekov Studio*
　Designer　　Theresa Paris
2.
　Client　　　*W.D. Burson + Associates.*
　Designer　　Jan Guarino
3.
　Client　　　*Annuncio Software*
　Designer　　Brian Jacobson
4.
　Client　　　*ShopEaze Systems*
　Designers　 Brian Jacobson, Anthony Luk
5.
　Client　　　*Leverage Studio*
　Designer　　Jan Guarino
6.
　Client　　　*Support Minds*
　Designers　 Brian Jacobson, Anthony Luk

7.
　Client　　　*Spectrum Photographic*
　Designer　　Brian Jacobson
8.
　Client　　　*ecotech*
　Designer　　Jan Guarino
9.
　Client　　　*Puget Sound Blood Center*
　Designer　　Lana R. Abrams
10.
　Client　　　*Light + Salt Presbyterian Church*
　Designer　　Wesley J. Su
11.
　Client　　　*DLC Leasing*
　Designer　　Jan Guarino
12.
　Client　　　*Holliswood Care Center*
　Designer　　Jan Guarino
13.
　Client　　　*Webline Designs*
　Designer　　Jan Guarino
14.
　Client　　　*Continuity Centers*
　Designer　　Jan Guarino
15.
　Client　　　*MediaStorytellers*
　Designer　　Brian Jacobson

191

The RESIDENCE at GLEN RIDDLE
ASSISTED LIVING

1.

2.

LORICH BUILDING CORP

3.

4.

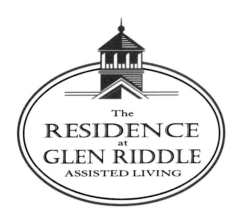

6.

7.

8.

9.

10.

11.

12.

13.

14.

15.

1 - 5		
Design Firm	**Guarino Graphics**	
6		
Design Firm	**Fusion Art Institute**	
7, 8		
Design Firm	**Davison Dietsch McCarthy**	
9 - 14		
Design Firm	**Laura Coe Design Assoc.**	
15		
Design Firm	**Belyea**	

1.
Client — *The Residence at Glen Riddle*
Designer — Jan Guarino

2.
Client — *Painted Pieces Studios*
Designer — Jan Guarino

3.
Client — *Lorich Building Corp.*
Designer — Jan Guarino

4.
Client — *Z Counsel LLC.*
Designer — Jan Guarino

5.
Client — *Bentley Properties*
Designers — Jan Guarino, Tara Gordon

6.
Client — *Youga*
Designers — Fumihiko Enokido, Hideaki Enokido

7.
Client — *Grand Rapids Area Center for Ecumenism*
Designer — Rachel Reenders

8.
Client — *Grace College*
Designers — Rachel Reenders, Kurt Dietsch

9.
Client — *Active Motif*
Designer — Thomas Richman

10.
Client — *Printing Industries Assoc.*
Designers — Laura Coe Wright, Thomas Richman

11.
Client — *Ballena Vista Farm*
Designers — Laura Coe Wright, Thomas Richman Tracy Castle

12.
Client — *ReturnView, Inc.*
Designer — Tracy Castle

13.
Client — *JNR, Inc.*
Designer — Ryoichi Yotsumoto

14.
Client — *Active Motif*
Designer — Thomas Richman

15.
Client — *Les Piafs*
Designers — Christian Salas, Kelli Lewis

1.

2.

3.

4. *Bird*Sight

5.

6. SIMON **LIVE MEDIA** N E T W O R K ™

7. THE Manhattan SOCIETY

8. Bove COMPANY

9.

10.

11.

12.

13.

14.

15.

195

1.

2.

3.

4.

5.

6.

7.

8.

9.

10.

11.

12.

13.

14.

15.

RECORDING
ACADEMY
MEMBERSHIP
AWARDS

1.

BODIES *in* **BALANCE**

2.

HUMANITY *through* **TECHNOLOGY**

3.

inVISION

4.

BINGHAM DANA

5.

CAPTIVATE™

6.

MICHIGAN

7.

BOSTON ARCHITECTURAL CENTER

8.

ROCKTAILS

9.

THE ARBORS
OF THOUSAND OAKS

10.

GK

11.

C I T I Z E N
S C H O O L S

12.

A?T

13.

30 adelaide e.

14.

15.

1.

2.

H·I·S INVESTMENTCONSULTING SERVICE GMBH

3.

4.

5.

6.

7.

8.

ADLER

9.

10.

GÖNNER+GAISSMEYER
PRÄZISIONSDREHTEILE

11.

HONBERG
SOMMER
2001

12.

Phillips
Gallery
of Fine
Art

13.

STADT
GEISINGEN
AN DER JUNGEN DONAU

14.

15.

1, 13
  Design Firm **The Wecker Group**
2 - 7, 9, 11, 12, 14
  Design Firm **revoLUZion-Studio für Design**
8, 10, 15
  Design Firm **Boelts Bros. Associates**
1.
  Client   *Highlands Inn Park Hyatt*
  Designer   Robert Wecker
2.
  Client   *HIS*
  Designer   Bernd Luz
3.
  Client   *Ba-Wü InLine-Cup*
  Designer   Bernd Luz
4.
  Client   *Paul Peschke*
  Designer   Bernd Luz
5.
  Client   *Cargo Team*
  Designer   Bernd Luz
6.
  Client   *take-off GewerbePark*
  Designer   Bernd Luz
7.
  Client   *Stadt NeBkirch*
  Designer   Bernd Luz

8.
  Client   *Nimbus Brewery*
  Designers Jackson Boelts, Brett Weber
9.
  Client   *Adler*
  Designer   Bernd Luz
10.
  Client   *Jackson Boelts*
  Designer   Jackson Boelts
11.
  Client   *Gönner+Gaissmeyer*
  Designer   Bernd Luz
12.
  Client   *Honberg Sommer*
  Designer   Bernd Luz
13.
  Client   *Phillips Gallery of Fine Art*
  Designer   Robert Wecker
14.
  Client   *Stadt Geisingen*
  Designer   Bernd Luz
15.
  Client   *Colorado Dance Festival*
  Designers Jackson Boelts, Eric Boelts

1.

2.

3.

4.

5.

6.

7.

8.

9.

10.

11.

12.

13.

14.

15.

1.

2.

3.

4.

5.

6.

7.

8.

water·color^{SM}

A Southern Coastal Landscape. **FLORIDA**

9.

10.

11.

12. A B A C U S

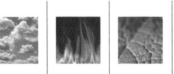

[J I V A C R E A T I V E]

14.

AKF
engineers

13.

15.

1.

2.

3.

4.

SURETHOUGHT

5.

photosphere studio

6.

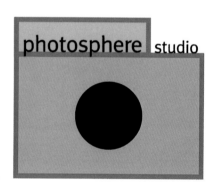

Spina Bifida
Association
of Dallas

7.

datamax

8.

 kedestra

9.

10.

:10m design

11.

The Health & Wellness Center
BY DOYLESTOWN HOSPITAL

12.

EXHALE™

13.

SOMA FOUNDATION

14.

1, 4, 12
Design Firm **Art 270 Inc.**
2, 10
Design Firm **Bailey Design Group**
3, 13, 14
Design Firm **Artemis Creative, Inc.**
5, 7, 8
Design Firm **Griffith Phillips Creative**
6, 9, 11
Design Firm **BBK Studio**

1.
Client   *West German BMW*
Designer   Sean Flanagan
2.
Client   *Goldenberg Candy Company*
Designers   David Fiedler, Steve Perry,
           Denise Bosler
3.
Client   *Bio-Rad Laboratories/Pure Water*
Designers   Wes Aoki, Betsy Palay,
           Mark Gallo
Illustrators   Gary Nusinow,
           Lisa Turan
4.
Client   *West German BMW*
Designer   Sean Flanagan
5.
Client   *Surethought, www.surethought.com*
Designer   Brian Niemann

6.
Client   *Photosphere*
Designers   Sharon Oleniczak,
           Michele Chartier
7.
Client   *Spina Bifida Association of Dallas*
Designer   Bo McCord
8.
Client   *Datamax, www.datamax.com*
Designer   Brian Niemann
9.
Client   *Kedestra*
Designers   Yang Kim, Kelly J. Schwartz
10.
Client   *H.J. Heinz Co.*
Designers   David Fiedler, Gary LaCroix,
           Man Hong Ling
11.
Client   *Mike Boysen*
Designer   Sharon Oleniczak
12.
Client   *The Health and Wellness Center*
           by Doylestown Hospital
Designers   John Opet, Carl Mill
13.
Client   *Exhale Therapeutics, Inc.*
Designers   Betsy Palay, Jim Temple,
           Mark Gallo
14.
Client   *Soma Foundation*
Designers   Betsy Palay, Wes Aoki

1.

2.

3.

4.

5.

6.

7.

8.

9.

Travel Health Resource
expert world travel advice

10.

11.

12.

Hearts and Hands
A CELEBRATION OF NEIGHBORS

13.

14.

1, 2
Design Firm **Deskey**
3, 4
Design Firm **Donald Makoski**
5, 6
Design Firm **Lux Design**
7
Design Firm **Trudy Cole-Zielanski Design**
8
Design Firm **Beth Singer Design**
9
Design Firm **Harbauer Bruce Nelson Design**
10
Design Firm **Design Moves, Ltd.**
11
Design Firm **Hansen Design Company**
12
Design Firm **Casper Design Group**
13
Design Firm **Mona MacDonald Design**
14
Design Firm **Whitney Edwards Design**

1.
Client   *Aqua Glass*
Designers   Siman Yan, Anauk Schofield,
            Timmy Chu
2.
Client   *Actron Mfg. Co.*
Designers   Siman Yan, Anauk Schofield
3.
Client   *Everest Broadband Networks*
Designer   Jane Heft

4.
Client   *Incentex Inc.*
Designer   Adam Peirce
5.
Client   *CoreMatter*
Designer   Michael Silva
6.
Client   *On the Page*
Designer   Laura Cary
7.
Designers   Trudy Cole-Zielanski,
            JMU Media Relations, Ann Hess
8.
Client   *The American Red Cross*
Designer   Chris Hoch
9.
Client   *Sanford Corporation*
Designer   Craig Harbauer
10.
Client   *Travel Health Resource*
Designers   Laurie Medeiros Freed,
            William Sprowl
11.
Client   *Nyhus Communications*
Designers   Pat Hansen, Jacqueline Smith
12.
Client   *Gazelle LLC*
Designers   Carolyn St. Jean, Bill Ribar
13.
Client   *Sisters of St. Joseph/Baden*
Designer   Mona MacDonald
14.
Client   *General Tanuki's Restaurant*
Designer   Charlene Whitney Edwards

C H I N E S E
I N F O R M A T I O N
C E N T R E

1.

Premarin

2.

3. **SALTWATER CITY**

4. **POS** TOUCH SCREEN SYSTEMS

sesame
workshop™

5.

GREYSTONE

6.

THOUSAND WORDS

7.

A I R L U M E
C A N D L E S

8.

9.

10.

a Contempo Design rental product

11.

VIPhysique

12.

the source

13.

14.

15.

CALLISON

1.

COLUMBIA WINERY

2.

All-LASER
THE NEW EDGE

3.

Lawson Design

4.

HONDA
Care

5.

RIGHT *home*

6.

ProVide

ATTRACTING THE BEST

7.

RIVERWALK
VISTA

8.

9.

AT EASTWALK COMMONS

10.

11.

12.

Rufino®
candles

13.

14.

15.

1.

2.

3.

4.

5.

6.

7.

8.

9.

10.

11.

wireless audio

12.

13.

the bakery and coffee bar

14.

CAMPAGNE

*French Country
Cuisine*

1.

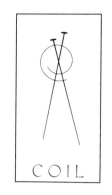

COIL

2.

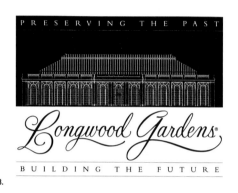

3.

SM

4.

Stone
wall
Vine
yard

5.

1978 - 1998

20

CELEBRATING 20 YEARS

6.

"squeak"

7.

THE HEAT IS ON!

8.

9.

10.

"meow"

SPIRIT SPORTS

11.

CATHOLIC Archdiocese OF ST. LOUIS

12.

MISS UNIVERSE 1983 ST. LOUIS U.S.A.

13.

14.

1.

2.

3.

4.

5.

6.

7.

8.

9.

10.

11.

12.

13.

2009

14.

15.

1, 2, 4, 8, 11, 12
Design Firm **Mark Oliver, Inc.**
3
Design Firm **J. Robert Faulkner Advertising**
5
Design Firm **Bailey Design Group**
6
Design Firm **Sayles Graphic Design**
7, 15
Design Firm **Full Steam Marketing & Design**
9
Design Firm **Harbauer Bruce Nelson Design**
10
Design Firm **Dixon & Parcels Associates, Inc.**
13
Design Firm **INC 3**
14
Design Firm **Concrete Design Communications Inc.**

1.
Client *Affinity Group*
Designer Mark Oliver
2.
Client *Organic Milling*
Designer Mark Oliver
3.
Client *The Red Thread*
Designer J. Robert Faulkner
4.
Client *Organic Milling—Back to Nature*
Designer Mark Oliver

5.
Client *Maxell*
Designers David Fiedler, Gary LaCroix, Man Hong Ling
6.
Client *1999 Iowa State Fair*
Designer John Sayles
7.
Client *Monterey Soda*
Designer Darryl Zimmerman
8.
Client *Ocean Beauty Seafood*
Designer Mark Oliver
9.
Client *IMC Salt*
Designer Larry Teolis
10.
Client *Dakota Halal Processing Company*
Designers Dixon & Parcels Associates, Inc.
11.
Client *Adrienne's Gourmet Food*
Designer Mark Oliver
12.
Client *Three Star Fish Company*
Designers Mark Oliver, Patty Driskel
13.
Client *Adam Dubin*
Designers Harvey Appelbaum, Nick Guarracino
14.
Client *Holt Renfrew*
Designer John Pylypczak
15.
Client *Fresh Express*
Designers Darryl Zimmerman, Gail Kabaker

1.

TOWERbank

2.

VISION &
mission

ONLINE
banking

COMMUNITY
connection

TOWERING
news

3.

eXtreme
THERAPY SEAT

4.

5.

BIG DEAL

6.

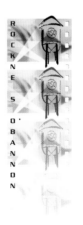

7.

wild
onion
CATERING

8.

HOLLYWOOD PHYSICAL THERAPY ASSOCIATES

9.

LEGEND SERIES
extreme

10.

THE
LIFE OF RYLEY
Manufacturers of Pet Accessories
Established 2000
USA

11.

just koz entertainment

12.

TYSZNA
GATUNEK
Q

13.

LAS
VEGAS

14.

15.

1 - 4, 10
Design Firm **Boyden & Youngblutt Advertising**
5, 11, 15
Design Firm **Wallace Church, Inc.**
6, 14
Design Firm **Mires**
7, 9, 12
Design Firm **Asylum**
8
Design Firm **Delphine Keim Campbell**
13
Design Firm **Parachute, Inc.**

1.
Client *Monark*
Designers Tim Favrote, Kelly Gayer

2.
Client *TowerBank*
Designer Jodi Matthias

3.
Client *TowerBank*
Designer Andy Boyden

4.
Client *MasterSpa*
Designers Chris Swymeler, Tim Favrote

5.
Client *Headline Productions*
Designers Wendy Church, Lucian Toma,
Pat Lore

6.
Client *Big Deahl*
Designers Jose Serrano, Miguel Perez

7.
Client *Rockne O'Bannon*
Designers Andrea Wynnyk, Jim Shanman

8.
Client *Wild Onion Catering*
Designer Delphine Keim Campbell

9.
Client *Hollywood Physical Therapy Assoc.*
Designers Andrea Wynnyk, Jim Shanman

10.
Client *MasterSpa*
Designers Chris Swymeler, Tim Favrote

11.
Client *The Life of Ryley*
Designers Wendy Church, Michael Scaraglino

12.
Client *Just Koz Entertainment*
Designers Andrea Wynnyk, Jim Shanman

13.
Client *Millennium Import Co.*
Designer Heather Cooley

14.
Client *Las Vegas Chamber of Commerce*
Designers Jose Serrano, Miguel Perez

15.
Client *Wallace Church, Inc.*
Designers Stan Church, Nin Glaister,
Lawrence Haggerty

1.

2.

3.

4.

5.

6.

7.

8.

222

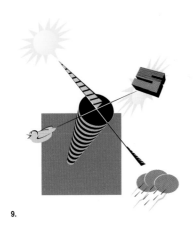

9.

LEAP™

10.

11.

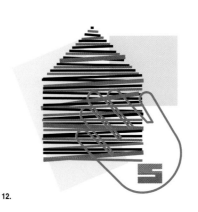

12.

13.

PASTA INDUSTRIES

14.

15.

1.

2.

3.

4.

5.

6.

7.

8.

224

9.

10.

11.

12.

13.

JIMMY AND DOUG'S

FARMCLUB.COM

14.

15.

1, 3, 4, 9, 15
Design Firm **Mike Salisbury LLC**
2, 5, 6, 8, 13
Design Firm **Zunda Design Group**
7
Design Firm **Stockdale Creative Marketing & Advertising**
10
Design Firm **Design Matters Inc!**
11
Design Firm **Addison**
12
Design Firm **Fiorentino Associates, Inc.**
14
Design Firm **Arnell Group**

1.
Client   *MGM Grand Hotel*
Designers   Devie Harven, Tor Naerheim
2.
Client   *B+G Foods, Inc.*
Designers   Todd Nickel, Charles Zunda
3.
Client   *Wings*
Designers   Mike Salisbury, Nina Weisbeck
4.
Client   *Panda Restaurant Group*
Designers   Mike Salisbury, Travis Page
5.
Client   *Makkos of Brooklyn, LTD*
Designers   Todd Nickel, Charles Zunda

6.
Client   *Newman's Own Inc.*
Designers   Charles Zunda, Todd Nickel
7.
Client   *Suzanne J. Stockdale*
Designers   Greg Brady, Irene Gurley, Judy Samet
8.
Client   *GAA Corporation*
Designer   Todd Nickel
9.
Client   *Brighton Avenue*
Designers   Mike Salisbury, David Walddin
10.
Client   *Cash Zone*
Designers   Stephen M. McAllister, Greg Cullen
11.
Client   *Domino's Pizza, Inc.*
Designers   Nick Bentley, Kraig Kessel
12.
Client   *EMR Systems Communication*
Designers   Lou Fiorentino, Andy Eng
13.
Client   *Reckitt Benckiser*
Designers   Pat Sullivan, Charles Zunda
14.
Client   *Farmclub.com*
Designers   Peter Arnell, Steven Hankinson, Mike Doyle
15.
Client   *20th Century Fox*
Designer   Don Marguez

1.

2.

3.

4.

5.

6.

7.

8.

West Ridge

CHURCH

9.

virtualteams.com

10.

11.

12.

LORD BISSELL BROOK

ATTORNEYS AT LAW

13.

Monroe Federal

Defining Local Banking

14.

1.

2.

Alphafuels

3.

4.

E R V I N G E O R G E O T V O S

5.

S A R A I D E

6.

7.

8.

9.

10.

11.

12.

capps|
digital studio

13.

EMPIRE THEATRES

**Entertainment.
We Set The Stage.**

14.

1, 6
    Design Firm **Primo Angeli Inc.**
2, 7
    Design Firm **Kirby Stephens Design**
3
    Design Firm **Miravo Communications**
4
    Design Firm **Blöch + Coulter Design Group**
5
    Design Firm **EGO Design**
8
    Design Firm **Hornall Anderson Design Works**
9, 12, 14
    Design Firm **McArthur Thompson & Law**
10, 11, 13
    Design Firm **Leo Burnett**
1.
    Client   *Church's Chicken*
    Designers Ariel Villasol, Peter Matsukawa,
              Kelson Mau
2.
    Client   *Autoindulgence*
3.
    Client   *Glofrog*
    Designer Justan Lustan
4.
    Client   *Blöch + Coulter Design Group*
    Designer Ellie Young Suh

5.
    Client   *EGO Design*
    Designer George Otvos
6.
    Client   *Saraide*
    Designer Ariel Villasol
7.
    Client   *Autoindulgence*
8.
    Client   *Twelve Horses*
    Designers Jack Anderson, Lisa Cerveny,
              Mary Chin Hutchison, Don Stayner
9.
    Client   *Sweet Jane's*
    Designers Rob Hansen, Jay Silver
10, 13.
    Client   *Capps Digital Studio*
    Designers Linda Goldberg, James Murphy
11.
    Client   *Gene Siskel Film Center*
    Designers Linda Goldberg, Jim Wood
12.
    Client   *Healthworld*
    Designer Rob Hansen
14.
    Client   *Empire Theatres*
    Designer Min Landry

1.

2.

3.

4.

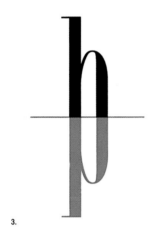

5.

6.

7.

8.

9.

project sunshine

bringing sunshine to a cloudy day[sm]

10.

take *the* lead!

Step into the light

11.

88

Sr

12.

BROADWAY

42 ST

NEW
2001
YORK
SPREE

13.

14.

15.

1.

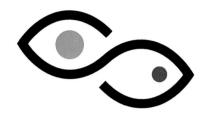

2.

NARADA ®

3.

portalplayer

4.

Advanced Medicine

5.

6.

7.

8.

9.

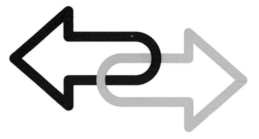

10.

11.

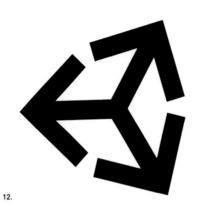

12.

MILLER'S MILLWORKS

13.

○

TELSEON

14.

TETRAGON

15.

1, 6, 9, 11, 13
Design Firm **Kraus/LeFevre Studios, Inc.**
2 - 5, 10, 12, 14, 15
Design Firm **Cahan and Associates**
7
Design Firm **Square Peg Graphics**
8
Design Firm **Paris Design Studio**

1.
Client *Xerox Corporation*
Designer Tracie J. Smith
2.
Client *Waterkeeper*
Designers Michael Braley, Bill Cahan
3.
Client *Narada*
Designers Sharrie Brooks, Bill Cahan
4.
Client *Portal Player*
Designers Michael Braley, Bill Cahan
5.
Client *Advanced Medicine*
Designers Bob Dinetz, Bill Cahan
6.
Client *Thermo Spectronic*
Designer Tracie J. Smith

7.
Client *Jim Decker, Rabbit's Movie Co.*
Designer Jack Jackson
8.
Client *Sonoma Marin Realty & Finance*
Designer Theresa Paris
9.
Client *Livingston County Development Group*
Designer Tracie J. Smith
10.
Client *Tumbleweed Communications*
Designers Bob Dinetz, Bill Cahan
11.
Client *Mossien Associates, Architects, P.C.*
Designer Tracie J. Smith
12.
Client *Veridical*
Designers Todd Simmons, Bill Cahan
13.
Client *Miller's Millworks*
Designer Tracie J. Smith
14.
Client *Telseon*
Designers Bob Dinetz, Bill Cahan
15.
Client *Tetragon*
Designers Craig Bailey, Bill Cahan

1.

2.

3.

4.

5.

6.

7.

8.

9.

10.

12.

11. RECHARGE

13.

14.

15.

MILLENNIUM

16.

17.

1.

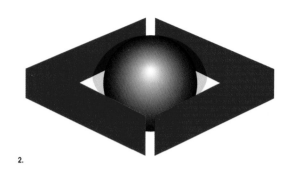

2.

3.

4.

5.

6.

7.

8.

DigitalMOBILEsoLUTiON

9.

10.

V I C T O R I A

S Y M P H O N Y

11.

Carmanah

12.

**THE CITY OF
VICTORIA**

13.

MACHIRIP

14.

PURDUE INTERNATIONAL CENTER FOR
ENTERTAINMENT TECHNOLOGY

15.

1, 5, 7, 8, 10 - 13
Design Firm **Trapeze Communications**
2 - 4, 6, 9, 14
Design Firm **Pete Smith Design**
15
Design Firm **Purdue University**

1.
Client   *Government Agents*
Designer   Mark Bawden
2.
Client   *Virtual Visit Presentations*
Designer   Pete Smith
3.
Client   *Design in Motion*
Designer   Pete Smith
4.
Client   *Venture Assistants*
Designer   Pete Smith
5.
Client   *Unity*
Designer   Mark Bawden
6.
Client   *Traffic Lite*
Designer   Pete Smith
7.
Client   *Art Gallery of Greater Victoria*
Designer   Mark Bawden

8.
Client   *BC's Family Fishing Weekend*
Designer   Mark Bawden
9.
Client   *Digital Mobile Solution*
Designer   Pete Smith
10.
Client   *Ministry of Women's Equality*
Designer   Mark Bawden
11.
Client   *Victoria Symphony*
Designer   Mark Bawden
12.
Client   *Carmanah Technologies*
Designer   Mark Bawden
13.
Client   *City of Victoria*
Designer   Mark Bawden
14.
Client   *Praxisoft*
Designer   Pete Smith
15.
Client   *Purdue International Center for
Entertainment Technology*
Designer   Li Zhang

237

1.

SANDIE JACOBS & ASSOCIATES

2.

3.

4.

5.

6.

7.

8.

9.

10.

11.

First
Baptist
Church

1799-1999

12.

13.

14.

15.

1
Design Firm **Boyden & Youngblutt Advertising**
2
Design Firm **Hiroshi Hamada Design Studio**
3 - 5, 8, 9, 11, 12
Design Firm **Kirby Stephens Design**
6, 10, 13 - 15
Design Firm **Shea**
7
Design Firm **Wittwer Industries**

1.
Client   *Lincoln Re Insurance*
Designers   Andy Boyden, Tim Favrote
2.
Client   *Sandie Jacobs & Associates*
Designer   Hiroshi Hamada
3.
Client   *KY Guild of Artists & Craftsmen*
4.
Client   *The Center for Rural Development*
5.
Client   *Sumerset Houseboats*
6.
Client   *Ooh Aah*
Designer   Pam McFerrin

7.
Client   *Kil Karney Mist*
Designer   Jason Wittwer
8.
Client   *Sumerset Houseboats*
9.
Client   *Bastin's Steakhouse*
10.
Client   *Marshall Field's—Mixed Greens*
Designer   Holly Utech
11.
Client   *East Kentucky Network*
12.
Client   *First Baptist Church*
13.
Client   *Select Comfort—Retail Store*
Designer   James Rahn
14.
Client   *Shea, Inc.*
Designers   Eric Fetrow, Viera Hartmannova
15.
Client   *Toys 'R' Us*
Designers   James Rahn, Jason Wittwer

239

1.

2.

AlphaLeader

3.

4.

6.

5.

7.

8.

240

9.

10.

11.

12.

13.

15.

1.

2.

3.

Monte Vista
small animal hospital

4.

5.

EAST BAY
corporate kids
INCORPORATED

6.

7.

8.

HEALTHY START
MODESTO CITY SCHOOLS

9.

HAFERS
HOME FURNISHINGS

10.

CENTRAL VALLEY IMAGING ASSOCIATES

11.

ACADEMY OF INFORMATION TECHNOLOGY

12.

RHODE ISLAND INTERLOCAL
 **The Trust**
RISK MANAGEMENT TRUST

13.

ARMADANI

14.

15.

1.

2.

3.

4.

5.

6.

7.

8.

9.

10.

11.

NUANCE

12.

Hulingshof

13.

14.

15.

1
Design Firm **FRCH Design Worldwide (Cincinnati)**

2, 3, 12
Design Firm **Landkamer Partners**

4
Design Firm **Wet Paper Bag Graphic Design**

5 - 11, 13 - 15
Design Firm **Buttgereit und Heidenreich**

1.
Client *Bostonian*
Designers Mike Brod, Dawn Wolf

2.
Client *Commerce One*
Designers Mark Landkamer, Gene Clark

3.
Client *ILOG*
Designers Mark Landkamer, Gene Clark

4.
Client *Texas Christian University Journalism Department*
Designer Lewis Glaser

5.
Client *C2 Team Coaching*
Designer Michael Buttgereit

6.
Client *Team. F*
Designers Michael Buttgereit, Karsten Kordus

7.
Client *VNR Verlag*
Designers Michael Buttgereit, Wolfram Heidenreich

8.
Client *ERF Evangeliumsrundfunk*
Designers Michael Buttgereit, Wolfram Heidenreich

9.
Client *Hoffnungszeichen (Sign of Hope)*
Designers Michael Buttgereit, Wolfram Heidenreich

10.
Client *Siebter Kontinent Interaktive Medien*
Designer Michael Buttgereit

11.
Client *Lindner*
Designers Michael Buttgereit, Wolfram Heidenreich

12.
Client *Nuance*
Designers Mark Landkamer, Gene Clark

13.
Client *Hulingshof*
Designer Wolfram Heidenreich

14.
Client *Simplify your Life*
Designers Michael Buttgereit, Wolfram Heidenreich

15.
Client *Innovo AG*
Designers Michael Buttgereit, Wolfram Heidenreich

1.

2.

3.

4.

5.

6.

7.

8.

9.

10.

11.

COMMUNICATIONS

12.

13.

uNetC•MMERCE™

UNIFIED INTERNET COMMERCE

14.

15.

1 - 5, 7, 8, 10, 13, 14
   Design Firm **Damion Hickman Design**
6, 11, 12
   Design Firm **Rolan Design Group**
9
   Design Firm **The Delor Group**
15
   Design Firm **Lee Communications, Inc.**

1.
Client	*Net Toaster*
Designer	Damion Hickman

2.
Client	*Agua Dulce Vineyards*
Designers	Damion Hickman, Matt Conger

3.
Client	*Symbion*
Designers	Damion Hickman, Leighton Hubbell

4.
Client	*MDC (North County Corp. Center)*
Designers	Damion Hickman, Conan Wang

5.
Client	*TVminder.com*
Designers	Damion Hickman, Alan Blount

6.
Client	*Chris Wendt, Inc.*
Designer	Douglas C. Rolan

7.
Client	*Media Vision*
Designers	Damion Hickman, Leighton Hubbell

8.
Client	*Extreme Sports Company*
Designer	Matt Conger

9.
Client	*Elan*
Designers	Chris Enander, Mike Owens, Kevin Wyatt

10.
Client	*TruSpeed MotorCars*
Designer	Damion Hickman

11.
Client	*Sports Car Service, Inc.*
Designer	Douglas C. Rolan

12.
Client	*Net Holdings, Inc.*
Designer	Douglas C. Rolan

13.
Client	*MDC (Origen Rail Center)*
Designers	Damion Hickman, Leighton Hubbell

14.
Client	*uNetCommerce*
Designer	Damion Hickman

15.
Client	*Capital Risk Concepts, Ltd.*
Designer	Bob Lee

1.

P H O E N I X

2.

CHILDREN'S HOME SOCIETY OF NORTH CAROLINA. EST. 1902

L I T T L E   R E D   S T O C K I N G   F U N D

3.

PETRA
LEADERSHIP
SOLUTIONS

4.

GREENSBORO
RADIOLOGY
THE MEDICAL IMAGING PROFESSIONALS

5.

J U D G E S | S T A F F I N G | G R O U P

Visionaries With Solutions

6.

THE
DESIGN
GROUP

I N T E G R A T E D

M A R K E T I N G

C O M M U N I C A T I O N S

7.

G R A P H I C   S Y S T E M S
I N T E R N A T I O N A L

8.

9.

WorkSmart

10.

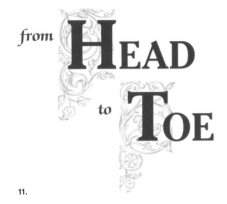

11.

12.

LEXINGTON ANESTHESIA

13.

a studio for home and garden

14.

INMARK

FURNITURE

15.

1.

2.

VASTERA

3.

4.

5.

6.

7.

8.

9.

ABINGTON
ART CENTER

10.

building together
DOYLESTOWN PRESBYTERIAN CHURCH 2001•2002

11.

D O R S Á L

12.

Old Tennent
Presbyterian Church
—— founded in 1692 ——

13.

14.

Millstone Coffee Dine & Dessert Café
Benefiting
MAKE A WISH

15.

White Hen

1.

INTERFACE

C H I L D R E N
F A M I L Y
S E R V I C E S

2.

Quantum**Shift**™

3.

KUMAI HARVEST™

4.

H Y O S H I N

5.

C Y N T R I C

6.

k i n e c t a ™

7.

The
Learning Community
I N S T I T U T E S

8.

Anchor Education

9.

10.

iospan
wireless™

11.

KICKFIRE ™

12.

cymbic

13.

Z H O N E

14.

15.

1
Design Firm **Addison**
2, 8, 9, 15
Design Firm **Barbara Brown**
Marketing & Design
3 - 7, 10 - 14
Design Firm **Cymbic**

1.
Client   *Clark Retail Enterprises:*
              White Hen Pantry
Designers   David Schuemann, Lisa Schuemann

2.
Client   *Interface*
Designer   Barbara Brown

3.
Client   *Quantum Shift*
Designers   Kénichi Nishiwaki, Ken Kubo,
              Yong An, David Nicol

4.
Client   *Kumai Harvest*
Designers   Kénichi Nishiwaki, Michael Fu-Ming,
              Amanda Ely, Joanna Dolby

5.
Client   *Hyogo Shinkin Bank*
Designers   Kénichi Nishiwaki, Ken Kubo,
              Ronald Blodgett

6.
Client   *Cyntric*
Designers   Kénichi Nishiwaki, Amanda Ely,
              Ken Kubo, Yong An

7.
Client   *Kinecta*
Designers   Kénichi Nishiwaki, Scott Jackson,
              Tracy Christensen

8.
Client   *TLCI*
Designer   Barbara Brown

9.
Client   *Anchor Education*
Designer   Barbara Brown

10.
Client   *Nutiva*
Designers   Kénichi Nishiwaki, Michael Fu-Ming

11.
Client   *Iospan Wireless*
Designers   Kénichi Nishiwaki, Ken Kubo,
              Yong An, Ronald Blodgett

12.
Client   *Kickfire*
Designers   Kénichi Nishiwaki, Ken Kubo,
              Ronald Blodgett

13.
Client   *Cymbic*
Designers   Kénichi Nishiwaki, Amanda Ely,
              Joanna Dolby, Michael Fu-Ming

14.
Client   *Zhone Technologies*
Designers   Kénichi Nishiwaki, Joanna Dolby,
              Amanda Ely, Michael Fu-Ming

15.
Client   *Ronald Reagan*
              Presidential Foundation
Designers   Barbara Brown, Amy Schneider,
              Jon A. Leslie

1. WIDE IDEA

THINK FASTER
THINK XEROX

2.

enfish. Onespace

3.

FALBROOKE
AT KRISTOPHER RANCH
SHEA HOMES

4.

THINK FASTER
THINK XEROX

5.

the Kiln Doctor Inc.

6.

newpak

USA

7.

CORK
SUPPLY
GROUP

8.

9.

10.

11.

THEMSWALK

12.

13.

SIXMAN**IAC**.

14.

15.

3.

2.

1.

4.

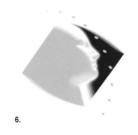

5.

6.

8.

7.

9.

10.

11.

12.

13.

14.

15.

1, 7, 9, 12, 13
Design Firm **The Benchmark Group**
2, 5, 6, 10, 14
Design Firm **Berni Marketing & Design**
3, 4, 8, 11, 15
Design Firm **Mastandrea Design, Inc.**

1.
Client   *Cincinnati Ballet*
Designer   John Carpenter
2.
Client   *Biscotti & Co.*
Designer   Carlos Seminario
3.
Client   *Half Moon Bay Pumpkin Run/*
              Senior Coast Siders
Designer   Mary Anne Mastandrea
4.
Client   *Texere*
Designer   Mary Anne Mastandrea
5.
Client   *Biscotti & Co.*
Designer   Carlos Seminario
6.
Client   *Berni Marketing & Design*
Designer   Carlos Seminario

7.
Client   *Cincinnati Ballet*
Designers   John Carpenter, Jen O'Shea
Illustrator   Ken Meade
8.
Client   *U.S.Advisor*
Designer   Mary Anne Mastandrea
9.
Client   *Cincinnati Ballet*
Designers   John Carpenter, Jen O'Shea
Illustrator   Ken Meade
10.
Client   *Acappella*
Designer   Peter Antipas
11.
Client   *Creagri, LLC*
Designer   Mary Anne Mastandrea
12.
Client   *Oil of Olay*
Designer   John Carpenter
Illustrator   Ken Meade
13.
Client   *Cincinnati Ballet*
Designers   John Carpenter, Jen O'Shea
Illustrator   Ken Meade
14.
Client   *Castleberry Snows*
15.
Client   *Get Real Girl, Inc.*
Designer   Mary Anne Mastandrea

1.

2.

3.

4.

5.

6.

7.

8.

9.

10. IAAPA

11.

12.

Digital Acorns, Inc.
Growing the Business of Technology

13.

14.

15.

1 - 4, 7, 10, 11, 14, 15
Design Firm **Kircher, Inc.**
5, 9, 12, 13
Design Firm **Vance Wright Adams & Associates**
6
Design Firm **Art 270, Inc.**
8
Design Firm **Dixon & Parcels Associates, Inc.**

1.
Client *Kids After School*
Designer Bruce E. Morgan
2.
Client *American Chemical Society*
Designer Ben Straka
3.
Client *American Chemical Society*
Designers Bruce E. Morgan, Ben Straka, John Frantz
4.
Client *Food Marketing Institute*
Designer Bruce E. Morgan
5.
Client *Rick John Inc.*
Designers Vance Wright Adams and Associates
6.
Client *Art 270, Inc.*
Designer Steve Kuttruff

7.
Client *SkyRocketer*
Designer Bruce E. Morgan
8.
Client *Winn-Dixie Stores, Inc.*
Designers Dixon & Parcels Associates, Inc.
9.
Client *Ben Franklin Technology Partners*
Designers Vance Wright Adams and Associates
10.
Client *International Association of Amusement Parks and Attractions*
Designer Bruce E. Morgan
11.
Client *Satellite Broadcasting & Communications Association*
Designer Ben Straka
12.
Client *E-Promotions Inc.*
Designers Vance Wright Adams and Associates
13.
Client *Digital Acorns, Inc.*
Designers Vance Wright Adams and Associates
14.
Client *Concept Interactive, Inc.*
Designer Bruce E. Morgan
15.
Client *National Assoc. of Home Builders*
Designer Bruce E. Morgan

1.

2.

3.

4.

5.

6.

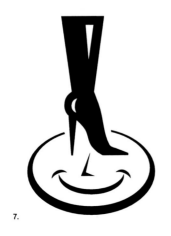

7.

8.

PROFESSIONAL SMILE SALON
First Impressions™

9.

HIXSON

10.

USTA
UNITED STATES
TELECOM
ASSOCIATION

11.

Federal Highway Administration
Office of Policy

12.

VentureForth

13.

LIFESCAN

14.

b4bpartner

15.

1, 4, 5, 8, 11 - 13
Design Firm **Sparkman + Associates**
2, 3, 6, 10, 14, 15
Design Firm **Gouthier Design, Inc.**
7
Design Firm **Greteman Group**
9
Design Firm **GOLD & Associates**

1.
Client   *Odyssey International*
Designer   Ryan Weible
2.
Client   *Paramount Hotel Group*
Designer   Jonathan Gouthier
3.
Client   *Grapevine Gourmet*
Designers   Jonathan Gouthier, Katerina Nadel
4.
Client   *Aprize Satellite*
Designer   Don Sparkman
5.
Client   *Blake Real Estate, Inc.*
Designers   Don Sparkman, Melanie Wilkins
6.
Client   *Elemental Solutions, Inc.*
Designers   Jonathan Gouthier, Marina
               Fagerstrom, Katerina Nadel

7.
Client   *ConnectCare*
Designers   Sonia Greteman, James Strange
8.
Client   *Goodwill Communications*
Designer   Don Sparkman
9.
Client   *First Impressions*
Designers   Keith Gold, Rob McFarland
10.
Client   *Hixson*
Designer   Jonathan Gouthier
11.
Client   *United States Telecom Association*
Designer   Don Sparkman
12.
Client   *Federal Highway Administration*
Designer   Don Sparkman
13.
Client   *VentureForth*
Designer   Don Sparkman
14.
Client   *Lifescan*
Designer   Jonathan Gouthier
15.
Client   *B4B Partner*
Designer   Jonathan Gouthier

1.

2.

waterpik

3.

ABACUS

4.

5.

VIGILANCE

6.

7.

8.

Exactly!

9.

10.

11.

12.

13.

mudd ®

14.

15.

1 - 3, 5, 7, 12, 14, 15
  Design Firm **Source/Inc.**
4, 6, 8 - 11, 13
  Design Firm **Mark Selfe Design**
1.
  Client   *Kraft Foods, Inc.*
2.
  Client   *Brunswick Recreation Group*
3.
  Client   *Waterpik Technologies*
4.
  Client   *Abacus Jewelry*
  Designer   Mark Selfe
5.
  Client   *World Kitchen*
6.
  Client   *Vigilance*
  Designer   Mark Selfe
7.
  Client   *Mirro Wearever*

8.
  Client   *Glorietta Elementary School*
  Designer   Mark Selfe
9.
  Client   *Exactly Vertical*
  Designer   Mark Selfe
10.
  Client   *Hatcher Press*
  Designer   Mark Selfe
11.
  Client   *Eurstyle.com*
  Designer   Mark Selfe
12.
  Client   *Nacional de Chocolates, S.A.*
13.
  Client   *NewMoon.com*
  Designer   Mark Selfe
14.
  Client   *Chattem, Inc. Consumer Products*
15.
  Client   *Valeo, Inc.*

solomiO

1.

2.

WETDAWG

3.

WHITEBOX advisors

4.

 Give2Asia

5.

NEWGROUND

6.

MYTALK

7.

8.

9.

10.

11. *Think outside.*

™

WallaWare

12.

FreshSeal™

13.

peoplebusinessnetwork™

People working better.

14.

15.

1, 2, 6, 7
Design Firm **Mortensen Design**
3
Design Firm **Funk & Associates**
4
Design Firm **Tilka Design**
5
Design Firm **Fifth Street Design**
8
Design Firm **Zunda Design Group**
9, 13
Design Firm **Bailey Design Group**
10, 12, 14
Design Firm **The People Business Network**
11, 15
Design Firm **Wilmer Fong + Associates**

1.
Client   *Solomio*
Designer   Michael McDaniel

2.
Client   *Futurus Bank*
Designers   P.J. Nidecker, Wendy Chon,
           Gordon Mortensen

3.
Client   *Wet Dawg*
Designer   Beverly Soasey

4.
Client   *Whitebox advisors*
Designer   Shannon Shriver

5.
Client   *Give2Asia*
Designers   J. Clifton Meek, Brenton Beck

6.
Client   *Newground Resources*
Designer   P.J. Nidecker

7.
Client   *MyTalk, Inc.*
Designer   P.J. Nidecker

8.
Client   *B+G Foods, Inc.*
Designers   Todd Nickel, Charles Zunda

9.
Client   *Dechert*
Designers   David Fiedler, Gary LaCroix

10.
Client   *Verizon Wireless*
Designer   Ken Thorlton

11.
Client   *Wilmer Fong + Associates*
Designer   Kean Hiroshima

12.
Client   *WallaWare, Inc.*
Designer   David Pfeiffer

13.
Client   *CPG Technologies*
Designers   David Fiedler, Ken Cahill,
           Ann Marie Malone

14.
Client   *The People Business Network*
Designer   Ken Thorlton

15.
Client   *Pleasanton Girls Soccer Association*
Designers   Steve Jeong, Nina Edwards

1.

2. EPOS | endless possibilites productions inc.

3.

4.

5.

6.

7.

8.

9. **Concept** Laboratories, Inc.

10. PIZZA COMPANY

11.

12. CLINIGEN

13.

14.

1, 2		
Design Firm	**EPOS, Inc.**	
3 - 14		
Design Firm	**What! design**	

1.
Client — *EPOS Concepts, Inc.*
Designer — Clifford Singontiko

2.
Client — *EPOS, Inc.*
Designer — Clifford Singontiko

3.
Client — *Bank Capital*
Designers — Damon Meibers, George Restrepo

4.
Client — *L2P Design*
Designers — Damon Meibers, Amy Strauch

5.
Client — *Clearcut Recording*
Designer — Damon Meibers

6.
Client — *Indy Girl*
Designers — Damon Meibers,
Aaron Carmisciano,
George Restrepo, Derek Aylward

7.
Client — *Songwriter Records*
Designers — Damon Meibers, Derek Aylward

8.
Client — *pmSolutions*
Designer — Damon Meibers

9.
Client — *Concept Laboratories, Inc.*
Designer — Damon Meibers

10.
Client — *Crazy Dough's Pizza Company*
Designers — Damon Meibers, Aaron Carmisciano

11.
Client — *Year Up*
Designers — Damon Meibers, Aaron Carmisciano

12.
Client — *Clinigen Inc.*
Designers — Damon Meibers, George Restrepo

13.
Client — *North Shore Swimwear*
Designers — Damon Meibers, Derek Aylward

14.
Client — *North Shore Swimwear—*
Aloha Swimwear
Designers — Damon Meibers, Derek Aylward

1.

2.

3.

4.

5.

6.

7.

8.

MAUZY
Management, inc.

9.

Tac's

PLACE

10.

SO?

11.

12.

STRATEGIC CHANGE MANAGEMENT

13.

NEW CHALLENGES 2000 NEW OPPORTUNITIES

YEAR

14.

1.

2.

adah oaks angus

3.

4.

5.

6.

270

7.

8.

9.

R E D
S Q U
A R E

10.

11.

MARQUIS
HOSPITALITY GROUP

12.

SOUTHEAST

MUTUAL INSURANCE
C O M P A N Y

13.

1 - 4, 6 - 9, 11 - 13
Design Firm **Sign Here, Inc.**
5, 10
Design Firm **Landesberg Design Associates**

1.
    Client   *Rockhound Trucking*
    Designer Melissa Shea
2.
    Client   *Rochester Floral & Gifts*
    Designer Melissa Shea
3.
    Client   *Adah Oaks Angus*
    Designer Lori Reynolds
4.
    Client   *Andy's Deli (Chafoulias Companies)*
    Designer Lori Reynolds
5.
    Client   *City Theatre*
    Designers Rick Landesberg, Joe Petrina
6.
    Client   *Blazing Needles*
    Designer Lori Reynolds

7.
    Client   *Amish Furniture Barn*
    Designer Melissa Shea
8.
    Client   *Frost Painting & Taping*
    Designer Lori Reynolds
9.
    Client   *Hamilton Builders*
    Designer Melissa Shea
10.
    Client   *Red Square Systems*
    Designers Rick Landesberg, Vicki Carlisle,
                Joe Petrina, Mike Savitski
11.
    Client   *Go-Fer Delivery*
              (Rochester Transportation Systems)
    Designer Lori Reynolds
12.
    Client   *Marquis Hospitality Group*
              (Chafoulias Companies)
    Designer Lori Reynolds
13.
    Client   *Southeast Mutual Insurance*
    Designer Melissa Shea

1.

Carleton

2.

 newmediary·com

3.

4.

 eCopy™

5.

6.

7.

8.

9.

10.

MY FIVE STAR CHEF

11.

D O R F

C A F É

12.

Contour Genesis
Ultrasonic Surgery System

13.

S

14.

MECHWERKS

15.

1.

2.

3.

5.

4.

6.

7.

8.

9.

10.

11.

12.

13.

14.

BlueBolt
NETWORKS

15.

1 - 14
Design Firm **Fleishman-Hillard Creative**
15
Design Firm **Alexander Isley Inc.**

1.
Client   *St. Louis Blues*
Designer   Buck Smith

2.
Client   *The Argent Hotel*
Designers   Kevin Kampwerth, Paul Scherfling

3.
Client   *Biomedical Systems, Inc.*
Designer   Kevin Kampwerth

4.
Client   *Fleishman-Hillard*
Designer   Buck Smith

5.
Client   *SBC Communications, Inc.*
Designer   Buck Smith

6.
Client   *Fleishman-Hillard*
Designer   Mike Montandon

7.
Client   *Washington Monarch Hotel*
Designer   Susan Gillham

8.
Client   *St. Louis Blues*
Designer   Buck Smith

9.
Client   *Sunnyhill Adventures*
Designers   John Senseney, Kevin Kampwerth

10.
Client   *San Francisco Giants*
Designer   Buck Smith

11.
Client   *Fleishman-Hillard*
Designer   Vicky Ho

12.
Client   *Hazelwood Central High School*
Designer   Buck Smith

13.
Client   *New York Urban League*
Designer   Ed Mantels-Seeker

14.
Client   *St. Louis Blues*
Designer   Buck Smith

15.
Client   *Bluebolt Networks*
Designers   Alexander Isley, Liesl Kaplan

PrimoGifts

1.

THE
COPLEY
CONDOMINIUM AND CLUB

2.

Tacoma
wine classic

3.

eCLIPS
Now
video
for
the
www

4.

JEWISH ORTHODOX
FEMINIST ALLIANCE
jofa

5.

TS
THE TAX STORE

6.

A Secret Garden

7.

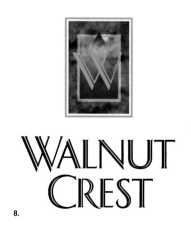

WALNUT CREST

8.

9.

10.

11.

12.

13.

14.

15.

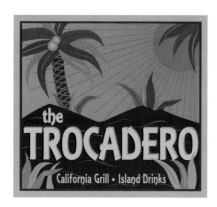

1.

2.

3.

4.

5.

6.

7.

8.

9.

10.

11.

12.

13.

14.

15.

(all)
Design Firm **On the Edge Design**

1.
   Client   *The Trocadero*
   Designers Jeff Gasper, Gina Mims

2.
   Client   *Blu Water Cafe*
   Designers Jeff Gasper, Tracey Lamberson

3.
   Client   *Jillian's—Hi Life Lanes*
   Designers Jeff Gasper, Gina Mims

4.
   Client   *L'Opera*
   Designers Jeff Gasper, Nicole Geiger-Brown

5.
   Client   *Platinum*
   Designers Jeff Gasper, Nicole Geiger-Brown

6.
   Client   *Mesquite Beach*
   Designers Jeff Gasper, Scott Jackson

7.
   Client   *JT Schmids*
   Designers Jeff Gasper, Gina Mims

8.
   Client   *Jillian's*
   Designers Jeff Gasper, Gina Mims

9.
   Client   *French 75*
   Designers Jeff Gasper, Gina Mims

10.
   Client   *Sea Grill*
   Designers Jeff Gasper, Nicole Geiger-Brown

11.
   Client   *Johns Incredible Pizza*
   Designers Jeff Gasper, Nicole Geiger-Brown

12.
   Client   *Caffee Panini*
   Designers Jeff Gasper, Nicole Geiger-Brown

13.
   Client   *Green Epstein Bacino*
   Designers Jeff Gasper, Nicole Geiger-Brown

14.
   Client   *BlueCat Cafe*
   Designers Jeff Gasper, Gina Mims

15.
   Client   *Sonomas Grill*
   Designers Jeff Gasper, Tracey Lamberson

1.

2.

3.

4.

5.

6.

A GREAT LOCATION

NEVER GOES OUT OF STYLE.

7.

8.

9.

10.

11.

12.

13.

KELLY, SCOTT & MADISON

14.

15.

1.

2.

3.

4.

5.

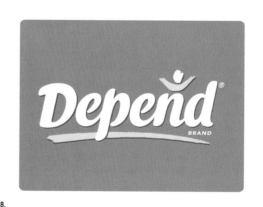

6.

7.

8.

9.

10.

11.

12.

13.

14.

15.

1, 2, 4, 5, 8, 10, 11, 14
Design Firm **Pedersen Gesk**
3, 7, 9
Design Firm **TGD Communications, Inc.**
6, 12, 13, 15
Design Firm **Karacters Design Group**

1.
Client　　*Schwan's Sales Enterprises—*
　　　　　Red Baron Brand
Designers　Rony Zibara, John Piper

2.
Client　　*Schwan's Sales Enterprises—*
　　　　　Schwan's Home Service Brand
Designers　Rony Zibara, Tracy Ghan

3.
Client　　*FireBoxx, LLC*
Designer　Gloria Vestal

4.
Client　　*Tone Brothers—Tone's Brand*
Designers　Rony Zibara, Beth Keys

5.
Client　　*Tone Brothers—Durkee Brand*
Designers　Rony Zibara, Beth Keys

6.
Client　　*CC Beverage Company*
Designers　Maria Kennedy, Matthew Clark

7.
Client　　*Society of Cable*
　　　　　Telecommunications Engineers
Designer　Gloria Vestal

8.
Client　　*Kimberly Clark—Depend Brand*
Designers　Rony Zibara, Scott Paul

9.
Client　　*Association of Government*
　　　　　Accountants
Designers　Chris Harrison, Jennifer Cedoz

10.
Client　　*Schwan's Sales Enterprises—*
　　　　　Tony's Brand
Designers　Rony Zibara, Scott Paul

11.
Client　　*Clorox—STP Brand*
Designers　Rony Zibara, John Piper

12.
Client　　*Spintopia*
Designers　Maria Kennedy, Roy White,
　　　　　Jeff Harrison

13.
Client　　*Cellex*
Designers　Maria Kennedy, Roy White,
　　　　　Nancy Wu

14.
Client　　*Pactiv—Hefty Brand*
Designers　Rony Zibara, John Piper

15.
Client　　*CC Beverage Company*
Designers　Maria Kennedy, Matthew Clark,
　　　　　Michelle Melenchuk

1.

2.

e.demartino design.

3.

SYNAVANT

4.

PRODUCTIONS

FIFTH SET

INTERNATIONAL, INC

5.

EAGLE PASS CAMINO REAL INTERNATIONAL BRIDGE

6.

HealthTrio ™

7.

1.

2.

3.

4.

STAND

Stress, anxiety and depression
affect one in four people.
Lack of understanding affects everyone.

5.

6.

7.

8.

THE IRON BED COMPANY

9.

evergreen

10.

Women. Men. Different. Equal.

11. Equal Opportunities Commission

MAC
MILITARY ASSISTANCE COMPANY

12.

Impact
Training Services, Inc.

13.

ELIZABETH FINN TRUST

14.

15.

1.

2.

3.

Living Well

Massage/Bodywork Professionals

4.

5.

BRITH SHALOM
RELIGIOUS SCHOOL

6.

7.

8.

9.

10.

hooch&pooch

11.

12.

13.

14.

15.

**Neuvo Latino
Restaurant & Night Club**

1.

2.

THE PEER
GROUP

PLASTIC SURGERY
CENTER

For Men & Women

3.

N E X T
M E D I A

4.

PLUM

5.

P R O J E C T

Advancement
Through
Education

6.

7.

New American Cuisine

8.

9.

10.

11.

12.

13.

14.

15.

1 - 3, 6 - 10, 12, 13
Design Firm **PM Design**
4, 5, 11, 14, 15
Design Firm **Made On Earth**

1.
Client *Babalu*
Designers Philip Marzo, Andrei Koribanics

2.
Client *B. Heaven*
Designer Philip Marzo

3.
Client *Peer Group*
Designer Philip Marzo

4.
Client *Next Media*
Designer Jay Vigon

5.
Client *Plum Productions*
Designer Jay Vigon

6.
Client *AY. PR.*
Designer Philip Marzo

7.
Client *24 by 7 Dating*
Designers Philip Marzo, Andrei Koribanics

8.
Client *Maize*
Designer Russ Mowry

9.
Client *South City Grill*
Designer Philip Marzo

10.
Client *Pomptonian Food Service*
Designers Philip Marzo, Andrei Koribanics

11.
Client *Post Logic Studios*
Designer Jay Vigon

12.
Client *Executive Solutions*
Designer Philip Marzo

13.
Client *B. Riccitelli Photography*
Designer Philip Marzo

14.
Client *Mohawk Productions*
Designer Jay Vigon

15.
Client *Necessary Evil*
Designer Jay Vigon

1.

2.

3.

EMPYREAN

4.

ROCHESTER
RAMP PARK

5.

6.

big blue sky, inc.

mercantec®

7.

8.

9.

10.

11.

12.

West Central Iowa
Solid Waste

Delivering Solid Waste Solutions...Together

13.

14.

15.

1.

2.

3.

Larry's Cedar River SEAFOOD & OYSTER BAR FRESH SEAFOOD

4.

Rēsendesign

5.

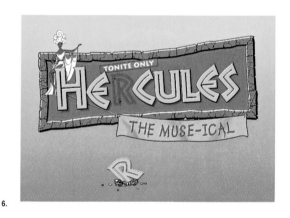

6.

7.

protegrity

8.

9.

10.

11.

BOB MOSHER MEMORIAL 5K RUN • MARCH 4, 2001

12.

13.

General Atlantic Partners

14.

15.

1, 3, 4, 6, 7, 9 - 13
　Design Firm **DeLisle + Associates**
2, 5, 8, 14, 15
　Design Firm **Rēsendesign**
1.
　Client　　Nico
　Designer　Marty Csercsevits
2.
　Client　　Intellego
　Designer　Ken Resen
3.
　Client　　Imagination Engineering
　Designer　Tom DeLisle
4.
　Client　　Larry's Cedar River
　Designer　Tim DeLisle
5.
　Client　　Rēsendesign Inc.
　Designers　Ken Resen, Alison Mann
6.
　Client　　Disney Cruise Line
　Designers　Jack Crouse IV, Tim DeLisle
7.
　Client　　Event Marketing & Mgmt. Int'l
　Designers　Marty Csercsevits, Michael Ruge

8.
　Client　　Protegrity, Incorporated
　Designer　Ken Resen
9.
　Client　　WDW Travel Industry Mktg.
　Designer　Marty Csercsevits
10.
　Client　　JacobDavis Productions
　Designer　Marty Csercsevits
11.
　Client　　Event Marketing & Mgmt. Int'l
　Designer　Marty Csercsevits
12.
　Client　　Cogistics, Inc.
　Designer　Michael Ruge
13.
　Client　　Church Street Entertainment
　Designer　Tim DeLisle
14.
　Client　　General Atlantic Partners
　Designer　Ken Resen
15.
　Client　　KM Management
　Designer　Ken Resen

1.

2.

G L O B A L

S E R V I C E S

3.

NAS PATUXENT RIVER

OPERATIONAL ENVIRONMENTAL
PLANNING OFFICE

4.

National Association
of Attorneys General

5.

6.

7.

8.

9.

10.

STONEHAVEN

11.

12.

13.

14.

15.

1.

2.

3.

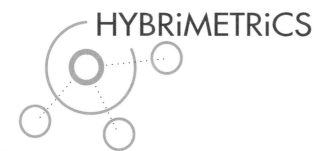

4.

5.

6.

7.

8.

9.

WESTERN
ASSOCIATED STUDENTS
BOOK*store*

10.

LISA ERSHIG INTERIORS

11.

6iXTH
STREET
WATERFRONT
PROPERTIES

12.

PACIFIC
MARINE
FOUNDATION

13.

BELLINGHAM
FESTIVAL *of* MUSIC

14.

TURNING POINT
realty advisors, LLC

15.

(all)		
Design Firm **MB Design**		
1.		
	Client	Walton Beverage
2.		
	Client	Diamond Ridge
3.		
	Client	James Alan Salon
	Designer	Ryin Kobza
4.		
	Client	Barkley Company
5.		
	Client	Hybrimetrics
6.		
	Client	Scentsations
7.		
	Client	Dawson Construction INC
8.		
	Client	Hotel Bellwether

9.		
	Client	Mark Bergsma Gallery
	Designer	Ryin Kobza
10.		
	Client	Western Washington University
11.		
	Client	Lisa Ershig Interiors
12.		
	Client	Haskell Corporation
13.		
	Client	Pacific Marine Foundation
14.		
	Client	Bellingham Festival of Music
	Designer	Ryin Kobza
15.		
	Client	Turning Point

1.

2.

3.

4.

5.

Invitrogen

6.

7.

1.

2.

3.

4.

5.

6.

7.

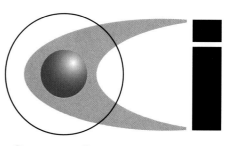

8.

9.

10.

11.

12.

13.

(all)
Design Firm **AKA Design, Inc.**

1.
Client *The Center for Transforming Worship*
Designer Mike Mullen

2.
Client *Ulysses S. Grant National Historic Site—Jefferson National Parks Association*
Designers John Ahearn, Richie Murphy

3.
Client *Gateway Arch—Jefferson National Parks Association*
Designers John Ahearn, Richie Murphy

4.
Client *MedEv LLC*
Designer Richie Murphy

5.
Client *The Daily Perc*
Designer J.R. Gain

6.
Client *Old Courthouse—Jefferson National Parks Association*
Designers John Ahearn, Richie Murphy

7.
Client *City of Hazelwood*
Designer Craig Martin Simon

8.
Client *Object Computing, Inc.*
Designer Mike Mullen

9.
Client *Kirkwood/Webster YMCA*
Designer John Ahearn

10.
Client *Recreation Station*
Designers Stacy Lanier, Craig Martin Simon

11.
Client *102nd Annual Session—American Association of Orthodontists*
Designer Mike Mullen

12.
Client *Illinois Special Olympics— East Central Area 9*
Designer Amy Ray

13.
Client *AKA Design, Inc.—15th Anniversary*
Designer Richie Murphy

1.

2.

3.

4.

5.

6.

7.

1, 4, 5
Design Firm **Liquid Agency, Inc.**
2, 3, 6
Design Firm **The Focus Group**
7
Design Firm **DavisPartners**

1.
Client   *Private Label*
Designers   Alfredo Muccino, Jill Steinfeld,
             Robert Wong

2.
Client   *Loomis, Fargo, & Company*
Designer   Kirk Davis

3.
Client   *Loomis, Fargo, & Company*
Designer   Kirk Davis

4.
Client   *Private Label*
Designers   Alfredo Muccino, Jill Steinfeld,
             Robert Wong

5.
Client   *Private Label*
Designers   Alfredo Muccino, Jill Steinfeld,
             Robert Wong

6.
Client   *Loomis, Fargo, & Company*
Designer   Kirk Davis
7.
Client   *State Colleges of Massachusetts*
Designers   Tom Davis, Ken Cool
opposite
Design Firm **[i]e design, Los Angeles**
Client   *Cal Fed Bank, Aspen Program*
Designers   Marcie Carson, Cya Nelson

1.

2.

The Power to Communicate.

VERMONT LIVING AT **QUECHEE LAKES**

3.

UNIVERSITY *of* OREGON
SUMMER
S E S S I O N

4.

UNIVERSITY *of* OREGON
SUMMER
S E S S I O N

5.

6.

PERCEPTION
COMMUNICATIONS, INC.

7.

UNIVERSITY *of* OREGON
SUMMER
S E S S I O N

8.

9.

10.

11.

12.

13.

14.

15.

1, 9, 12, 13
Design Firm **Design North**
2, 7, 11, 14, 15
Design Firm **[i]e design, Los Angeles**
3, 6
Design Firm **DavisPartners**
4, 5, 8, 10
Design Firm **Funk & Associates**

1.
Client *Calm Air*
Designer *Volker Beckmann*
2.
Client *Media Pointe*
Designers *Marcie Carson, Cya Nelson*
3.
Client *Quechee Lakes*
Designers *Tom Davis, Chuck Taylor*
4.
Client *UO Summer Session*
Designer *Beverly Soasey*
5.
Client *UO Summer 2001-B*
Designer *Beverly Soasey*
6.
Client *Redington LLC*
Designers *Tom Davis, Glenn Soulia*

7.
Client *Perception Communications, Inc.*
Designers *Marcie Carson, Amy Klass*
8.
Client *UO Summer 2001-A*
Designer *Beverly Soasey*
9.
Client *Northwest Development Corporation*
Designer *Volker Beckmann*
10.
Client *Extraordinary Work Group*
Designer *Beverly Soasey*
11.
Client *Metromedia Technologies*
Designers *Marcie Carson, Richard Haynie*
12.
Client *Burntwood Hotel*
Designer *Volker Beckmann*
13.
Client *Goldsand Adventures*
Designer *Volker Beckmann*
14.
Client *Da Vita Inc.*
Designers *Marcie Carson, Cya Nelson*
15.
Client *Gilad Development*
Designers *Marcie Carson, Cya Nelson*

THOMPSON
Chiropractic
C·L·I·N·I·C

1.

2.

3.

Collegiate
Health Care

4.

early
INSURANCE

5.

annual color
exterior design

6.

Secret

7.

1, 5
Design Firm **Design North**

2
Design Firm **Logos Identity by Design Limited**

3, 6
Design Firm **cottrill design**

4
Design Firm **DavisPartners**

7
Design Firm **Fixgo Advertising (M) Sdn Bhd**

1.
Client   *Thompson Chiropractic Clinic*
Designer   Volker Beckmann

2.
Client   *TDP Inc.*
Designer   Gabriella Sousa

3.
Client   *urban expositions*
Designer   Allison Cottrill

4.
Client   *Collegiate Health Care*
Designers   Tom Davis, Ken Cool

5.
Client   *Early Insurance*
Designer   Volker Beckmann

6.
Client   *Annual Color*
Designer   Allison Cottrill

7.
Client   *Tohtonku Sdn Bhd*
Designer   FGA Creative Team

opposite
Design Firm **Mires**
Client   *The Yellow Pages*
Designers   Jose Serrano, Brian Fandetti,
               Miguel Perez

2.

7.

5.

3.

1.

ANDERSON
ASSOCIATES

6.

4.

8.

9.

10.

11.

THE TORONTO HOSPITAL

12.

13.

14.

15.

1 - 9
Design Firm **ImagineGrafx**
10 - 15
Design Firm **Logos Identity by Design Limited**

1.
Client   *Anderson Associates*
Designers   Kyle Maxwell, Stephen Guy

2.
Client   *Thrasher Sharks Street Hockey*
Designer   Stephen Guy

3.
Client   *OCI Ministries Colorado*
Designer   Kyle Maxwell

4.
Client   *South Valley Christian Church*
Designer   Stephen Guy

5.
Client   *Prism Insurance & Financial*
Designer   Stephen Guy

6.
Client   *Global Ministries*
Designers   Stephen Guy, Kyle Maxwell

7.
Client   *Imagine Graphics*
Designer   Stephen Guy

8.
Client   *Victoria Harris Legal Search*
Designer   Stephen Guy

9.
Client   *Morazan Roofing*
Designer   Stephen Guy

10.
Client   *Quality Cracker & Cookie Company*
Designers   Anna Volpentesta, Franca DiNardo

11.
Client   *Actra Toronto Performers*
Designer   Gabriella Sousa

12.
Client   *The Toronto Hospitals*
Designer   Brian Smith

13.
Client   *The Great Atlantic & Pacific Company of Canada*
Designer   Anna Volpentesta

14.
Client   *Obsidian Theatre Company*
Designers   Gabriella Sousa, Brian Smith

15.
Client   *Parmalat Canada*
Designers   Anna Volpentesta, Franca DiNardo

1.

2.

Queen City *Reprographics*

3.

GUARDIAN'S FALL SALES CAMPAIGN

4.

O'BANNON CREEK

Golf Club

5.

ITRONIX ®

6.

7.

1
Design Firm **Liquid Agency**
2, 3, 5
Design Firm **Interbrand Hulefeld**
4, 7
Design Firm **Fiorentino Associates, Inc.**
6
Design Firm **Klündt Hosmer Design**
1.
Client *Music in the Park*
Designers Alfredo Muccino, Joshua Swanbeck
2.
Client *Evenflo (Gerry Brand)*
Designer Bart Laube
3.
Client *Queen City Reprographics*
Designer Christian Neidhard
4.
Client *Guardian Life Insurance Co.*
Designer Michael C. Toomey

5.
Client *O'Bannon Creek*
Designers Jodi Sena, Tom Tekulve
6.
Client *Itronix*
Designers Darin Klündt, Henry Ortega
7.
Client *Guardian Life Insurance Co.*
Designer Andy Eng
opposite
Design Firm **Design North**
Client *River Cabaret*
Designer Volker Beckmann

1.

2.

WARP & WOOF

ADVISORS

3.

ann loureiro

4.

SALON

5.

6.

P. Wexford's Pub

7.

SAMARITAN
VILLAGE

8.

INTER-FAITH MINISTRIES

REACHING OUT TO THOSE IN NEED...

9.

Four Seasons Farms

10.

Marcia Herrmann Design

11.

AN INTERNET COFFEE BAR

12.

WristWand™

13.

SAN FRANCISCO

14.

15.

1 - 14			8.		
Design Firm	**Marcia Herrmann Design**			Client	Samaritan Village
15				Designer	Marcia Herrmann
Design Firm	**Funk & Associates**		9.		
1.				Client	Interfaith Ministries
	Client	Brunos Peppers		Designer	Marcia Herrmann
	Designer	Marcia Herrmann	10.		
2.				Client	Four Seasons Farms
	Client	Stanislaus County Foundation		Designer	Marcia Herrmann
	Designer	Marcia Herrmann	11.		
3.				Client	Marcia Herrmann Design
	Client	Warp & Woof		Designer	Marcia Herrmann
	Designer	Marcia Herrmann	12.		
4.				Client	Wired
	Client	Ann Loureiro		Designer	Marcia Herrmann
	Designer	Marcia Herrmann	13.		
5.				Client	Wristwand
	Client	Salon Salon		Designer	Marcia Herrmann
	Designer	Marcia Herrmann	14.		
6.				Client	Hotel Rex
	Client	Michael Hat Farming		Designer	Marcia Herrmann
	Designer	Marcia Herrmann	15.		
7.				Client	iHorses
	Client	P. Wexfords Pub		Designers	Beverly Soasey, Alex Wijnen
	Designer	Marcia Herrmann			

315

7.

1.

2.

3.

4.

5.

6.

1
  Design Firm **Spine Design**
2, 5, 6
  Design Firm **Tieken Design &**
  Creative Services
3, 4
  Design Firm **Primo Angeli Inc.**
7
  Design Firm **Julia Tam Design**
1.
  Client   *Wizards Family Center*
  Designer Laurie Shattuck
2.
  Client   *Lumature*
  Designer Rik Boberg
3.
  Client   *MyRoad.com*
  Designer Toby Sudduth
4.
  Client   *DevX*
  Designer Toby Sudduth
5.
  Client   *Subway*
  Designers Fred E. Tieken, Lisette Sacks

6.
  Client   *Subway*
  Designers Fred E. Tieken, Lisette Sacks
7.
  Client   *Tao Tao*
  Designer Julia Chong Tam
opposite
  Design Firm **The Douglas Group**
  Client   *The Houston Astros' Enron Field*
  Designers Frank Douglas, Juliana Marek,
            Duane Farthing
  Photographer
            Aker/Zvonkovic

1.

2.

3.

4.

5.

6.

7.

8.

9.

TRELLIS

10.

agora

11.

TIPTOP
Since / Depuis
1909

12.

NEXUS

13.

14.

15.

1		
Design Firm **Funk & Associates**		
2 - 15		
Design Firm **Karo (Toronto) Inc.**		
1.		
Client	*Garden Architecture*	
Designer	Alex Wijnen	
2.		
Client	*Sprint Canada*	
Designers	Michael Malloy, Shawn Rasmussen	
3.		
Client	*Kolter Developments*	
Designers	Paul Browning, Iwona Sowinski	
4.		
Client	*CryoCath Technologies Inc.*	
Designers	Paul Browning, Derek Wessinger, Shawn Rasmussen	
5.		
Client	*Sara Thompson Asso.*	
Designers	Paul Browning, Josie Sena	
6.		
Client	*Universe2U*	
Designers	Paul Browning, Paola Beltrame	
7.		
Client	*The Learning Alliance*	
Designers	Paul Browning, Iwona Sowinski	

8.	
Client	*Hospitals of Ontario Pension Plan*
Designers	Michael Malloy, Joseph Chan, Steve Valentim
9.	
Client	*City of Oakville*
Designers	Paul Browning, Michael Malloy, Iwona Sowinski
10.	
Client	*Trellis Corporation*
Designers	Michael Malloy, Paola Beltrame
11.	
Client	*Oshawa Food Group*
Designers	Paul Browning, Peter Baker
12.	
Client	*Tip Top Tailors*
Designers	Michael Malloy, Maria Arshavsky
13.	
Client	*Nexus Group International*
Designers	Michael Malloy, Derwyn Goodall
14.	
Client	*Polus Center*
Designer	Mike Melnyk
15.	
Client	*Humber College*
Designers	Paul Browning, Nuno Ferreira, Derek Wessinger

1.

2.

3.

4.

5.

6.

7.

1, 3, 5, 7
Design Firm **Epstein Design Partners, Inc.**
2
Design Firm **Calori & Vanden-Eynden**
4, 6
Design Firm **Design North, Inc.**
1.
Client *Richland Development Corp.*
Designers Marla Gutzwiller, Jileen Coy
2.
Client *Greater Jamaica Dev. Corp*
Designers David Vanden-Eynden,
Marisa Schulman
3.
Client *Richland Development Corp.*
Designers Marla Gutzwiller, Jileen Coy
4.
Client *Fox River Paper Co.*
Designer Mark Topczewski
5.
Client *Richland Development Corp.*
Designers Marla Gutzwiller, Jileen Coy

6.
Client *Wellmark*
Designer Patrick Cowan
7.
Client *Richland Development Corp.*
Designers Marla Gutzwiller, Jileen Coy
opposite
Design Firm **Hornall Anderson Design Works**
Client *Grapefinds*
Designers Jack Anderson, Lisa Cerveny,
Mary Chin Hutchison,
Jana Wilson Esser, Gretchen Cook

PARK 5

BISTRO

1.

2.

ClipperNet
CORPORATION

3.

4.

café
YUMM!

5.

Arlie & Company
LAND AND INVESTMENTS

6.

7.

8.

ShelterCare
Hope is here.

9.

UNIVERSITY
HOUSING
OF OREGON

10.

Chambers
P R O D U C T I O N S

11.

OTN
Oregon Transportation Network

12.

EUGENE PUBLIC LIBRARY FOUNDATION

13.

Summer Oaks
B U S I N E S S   P A R K

14.

DEQ

State of Oregon
Department of
Environmental
Quality

15.

(all)
Design Firm **Funk & Associates**

1.
Client	*Park 5 Bistro*
Designer	Beverly Soasey

2.
Client	*Intuigy*
Designer	Lada Korol

3.
Client	*Clippernet*
Designer	Beverly Soasey

4.
Client	*Clovis*
Designer	Chris Berner

5.
Client	*Café Yumm*
Designer	Chris Berner

6.
Client	*Arlie & Company*
Designer	Beverly Soasey

7.
Client	*Avolaré*
Designer	Chris Berner

8.
Client	*Wings Bar & Grille*
Designer	Chris Berner

9.
Client	*Sheltercare*
Designers	Alex Wijnen, Lada Korol

10.
Client	*UO Housing*
Designer	Beverly Soasey

11.
Client	*Chambers Production*
Designer	Kathleen Heinz

12.
Client	*Oregon Transportation Network*
Designer	Beverly Soasey

13.
Client	*Eugene Public Library Foundation*
Designers	Kathleen Heinz, Beverly Soasey

14.
Client	*Summer Oaks*
Designers	Chris Berner, Beverly Soasey

15.
Client	*DEQ*
Designers	Chris Berner, Beverly Soasey

1.

2.

3.

4.

5.

6.

7.

1
    Design Firm **Inca Tanvir Advertising Limited**
2, 7
    Design Firm **Meteor Creative**
3
    Design Firm **Bremmer & Goris Communications**
4, 5
    Design Firm **Design North, Inc.**
6
    Design Firm **Gregory Gersch**

1.
    Client   *Dubai Flying Association*
    Designer   Suresh Pawar
2.
    Client   *Meteor Creative*
    Designers   Daniel Conlan, Gregory Gersch
3.
    Client   *World Wildlife Fund International*
    Designer   Gregory Gersch
4.
    Client   *Search Dog, Inc.*
    Designer   Patrick Cowan

5.
    Client   *Car X Service Systems, Inc.*
    Designer   Mark Topczewski
6.
    Client   *Frank Parsons Paper*
    Designer   Gregory Gersch
7.
    Client   *EnterActing*
    Designers   Gregory Gersch, Daniel Conlan
opposite
    Design Firm **Liquid Agency, Inc.**
    Client   *Liquid Agency, Inc.*
    Designers   Alfredo Muccino, Joshua Swanbeck

1.

2.

3.

4.

5.

6.

7.

8.

handwashingforlife™

9.

10.

Planet Cargo
The smartest move on the planet

11.

ShopAllAmerica.com™

12.

S2k

13.

DreamDance

14.

The Northern Lights Theater
— AT POTAWATOMI BINGO CASINO —

15.

1.

2.

3.

Collage

4.

MUSEUM OF NEW ART

5.

the world's best investors found here

marketocracy™

6.

boogie board

7.

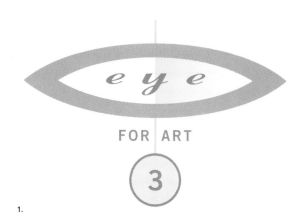

1.

2.

3.

4.

carpe!centum

5.

ChicagoBroker.com

6.

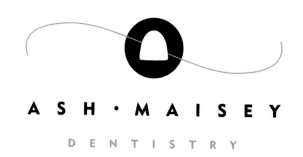

7.

8.

9.

FRIENDS · OF
SIGNAL HILL
CULTURAL ARTS

10.

11.

12.

13.

bella forma
pilates studio
FULL BODY FLEX & STRENGTH TRAINING

14.

15.

1, 4
Design Firm **Skidmore, Inc.**
2, 3, 6
Design Firm **Pivot Design, Inc.**
5, 7
Design Firm **Richards & Swensen**
8 - 15
Design Firm **Simple Green Design**

1.
Client   *Detroit Institute of Art*
Designer   John Latin

2.
Client   *Alzheimer's Association*
Designer   Jennifer Stortz

3.
Client   *Uppercase Books, Inc.*
Designers   Brock Haldeman, Liz Haldeman

4.
Client   *Village Green Communities*
Designer   Robert Nixon

5.
Client   *Dunn Communication*
Designer   William Swensen

6.
Client   *ChicagoBroker.com*
Designer   Don Emery

7.
Client   *Dunn Communications*
Designer   William Swensen

8.
Client   *Shades of Light Studio*
Designer   Wesley J. Su

9.
Client   *Academy of Animation & Digital Art*
Designer   Russ Scott
Illustrator   Norman Lao

10.
Client   *Friends of Signal Hill Cultural Arts*
Designer   Wesley J. Su

11.
Client   *Simple Green*
Designers   Russ Scott, Mike Brower

12.
Client   *Simple Green*
Designers   Russ Scott, Mike Brower

13.
Client   *Natsume Koi Farm*
Designer   Wesley J. Su

14.
Client   *Bella Firma Pilates Studio*
Designers   Wesley Su, Mike Brower

15.
Client   *R.O.C.K. Institute*
Designers   Mike Brower, Russ Scott
Illustrators   Norman Lao, Russ Scott

GATEWAY TO OPPORTUNITY
STAIRWAY TO EXCELLENCE

1.

2.

e st @ r t

3.

QI HE TANG

4.

5.

6.

1
Design Firm **Rickabaugh Graphics**
2, 5, 6
Design Firm **Nesnadny + Schwartz**
3, 4
Design Firm **Ukulele Design
Consultants Pte Ltd**
1.
Client   *Morgan State University*
Designer   Dave Cap
2.
Client   *Crawford Museum of
Transportation and Industry*
Designers   Greg Oznowich,
Jennifer Hargreaves
3.
Client   *S & I Technologies Pte Ltd*
Designers   Kim Chun Wei, Lynn Lim
4.
Client   *Qi He Tang*
Designers   Verna Lim, Lynn Lim

5.
Client   *The International Spy Museum*
Designers   Tim Lachina, Greg Oznowich
6.
Client   *Perkins School for the Blind*
Designer   Greg Oznowich
opposite
Design Firm **Smith Design Associates**
Client   *Good Humor Breyers*
Designer   James C. Smith

1.

2.

3.

4.

5.

6.

7.

8.

9.

10.

Portobellos
ITALIAN CUISINE

11.

Lighthouse Pointe

12.

13.

14.

15.

1, 4, 5, 8, 14
Design Firm **Wizards of the Coast (In-House)**
2, 3, 7, 9 - 12, 15
Design Firm **ID8/RTKL Associates Inc.**
Client *Harbour Plaza*
Hotel Management Inc.

6, 13
Design Firm **ID8/RTKL Associates Inc.**
Client *The Mills Corporation*

1.
Client *Showdown Sports*
Designers Shauna Wolf-Narciso,
John Casebeer

2.
Designers Thom McKay, Jill Popowich,
John Scheffel, Jeff Wotoweic

3.
Designers Thom McKay, Jill Popowich

4.
Client *NFL Showdown Sports*
Designers Shauna Wolf-Narciso,
John Casebeer

5.
Client *NBA Showdown Sports*
Designers Shauna Wolf-Narciso,
John Casebeer

6.
Designers Charlie Greenawalt, Molly Miller,
Greg Rose, Jennifer Cardinal

7.
Designers Thom McKay, Jill Popowich

8.
Client *MLB Showdown Sports*
Designers Shauna Wolf-Narciso,
John Casebeer

9.
Designers Thom McKay, Keith Kellner,
John Scheffel, Jill Popowich

10.
Designers Thom McKay, Greg Rose

11.
Designers Thom McKay, Pornprapha
Phatanateacha, John Scheffel

12.
Designers Thom McKay, Jessica Koman

13.
Designers Charlie Greenawalt, Greg Rose,
Frank Christian

14.
Client *MTG Protour*
Designers Jeremy Bills, John Casebeer

15.
Designers Thom McKay, John Scheffel

1.

2.

3.

e.**de**martino
de**sign.**

4.

moscato design

5.

2001

SUMMER OUTING

6.

75 Years
RADIO CITY
ROCKETTES

7.

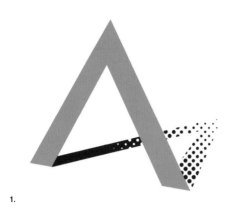

1.

THE CITY OF
LAKE FOREST
CHARTERED 1861

2.

VISUAL®
insights

3.

THE
SUGAR ASSOCIATION

4.

5.

AquariusAquarium
INSTITUTE

6.

Sutton Group
SOLUTIONS FOR SOCIAL CHANGE

7.

8.

9.

10.

MANIFEST
INTERNATIONAL LLC
A Media Finance Consultancy

11.

WATER'S EDGE GARDENING
Wetscape Design

12.

13.

14.

15.

1.

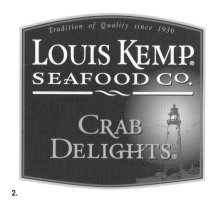

2.

CLEAN

3.

4.

THE PRINTWORKS

5.

ALGARVESHOPPING

6.

Bonaire
Parque Comercial y de Ocio

7.

1, 3
Design Firm **Motter-Design**
2
Design Firm **Source/Inc.**
4 - 7
Design Firm **RTKL—UK Ltd**
1.
Client   *Stiftung Maria Ebene*
Designers   Othmar Motter, Siegmund Motter
2.
Client   *Louis Kemp Seafood*
3.
Client   *Stiftung Maria Ebene*
Designers   Othmar Motter, Siegmund Motter
4.
Client   *Continente*
Designer   Glyn Rees
5.
Client   *Richardsons*
Designer   Glyn Rees
6.
Client   *Sonae Imobiliária*
Designer   Glyn Rees

7.
Client   *Grupo Riofisa*
Designer   Glyn Rees
opposite
Design Firm **Volan Design**
Client   *DataPlay*
Designer   Michele Braverman

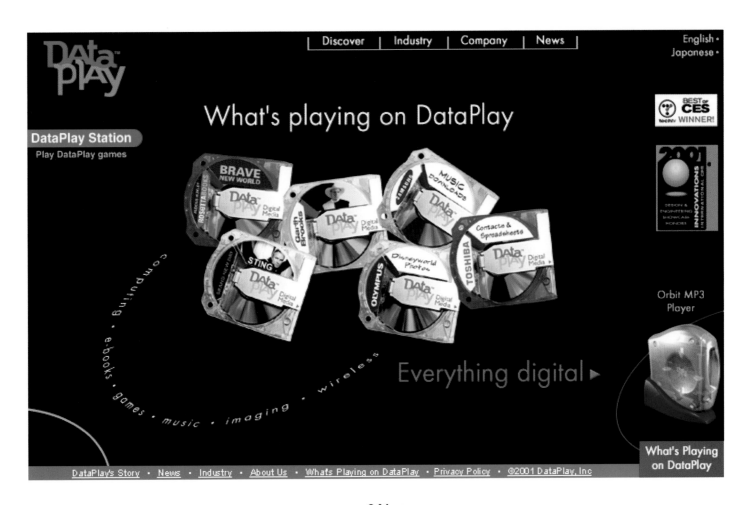

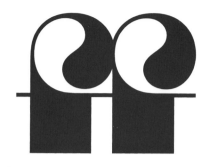

1.

2.

3.

4.

5.

6.

SENIOREN
BEIRAT

7.

8.

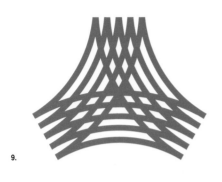

9.

10.

11.

12.

AUSTRIAN EMBROIDERIES

13.

14.

15.

(all)
Design Firm **Motter-Design**

1.
   Client   *Fellner-Fashion*
   Designer Othmar Motter

2.
   Client   *Seepark Hard*
   Designer Othmar Motter

3.
   Client   *Frick—Gartenbaubedarf, Vaduz*
   Designer Othmar Motter

4.
   Client   *Die Stütze*
             (Jugendhilfswerk in Götzis, Austria)
   Designer Othmar Motter

5.
   Client   *Spielwaren-Roth*
   Designers Peter Motter, Othmar Motter

6.
   Client   *Dr. Hedwig Birnbaumer*
   Designers Peter Motter, Othmar Motter

7.
   Client   *Senioren-Beirat*
             der Vorarlberger Landesregierung
   Designer Othmar Motter

8.
   Client   *Österreichische Reitsport-Union*
   Designer Othmar Motter

9.
   Client   *Mühlbauer, headwear*
             (Wien, Austria)
   Designer Othmar Motter

10.
   Client   *Wasserkraftwerk Egg*
   Designer Othmar Motter

11.
   Client   *Sportverein Salzbach*
   Designer Othmar Motter

12.
   Client   *Bund Österreichischer Sportvereine*
   Designer Othmar Motter

13.
   Client   *Austrian Embroideries*
   Designer Othmar Motter

14.
   Client   *Internationaler Bodensee Club*
   Designer Othmar Motter

15.
   Client   *Vorarlberger Handels-Zentrum AG*
   Designer Othmar Motter

1.

Y O U T H
M U S E U M
E X H I B I T
COLLABORATIVE

2.

3.

BENCHMARK ◆ HOSPITALITY

4.

5.

6.

7.

1.

2.

3.

4.

5.

6.

7.

8.

9.

10.

11.

12.

13.

1.

VAL VISTA MEADOWS

2.

harter & associates

3.

4.

Leadership Café

™

5.

CAPS
RESEARCH

6.

7.

1 - 7
Design Firm **Spark Design**
1.
Client   *Avnet/Hallmark*
Designer Vince Adam
2.
Client   *Monterey Homes*
Designer Joe Gunsten
3.
Client   *Harter and Associates*
Designer Rik Boberg
4.
Client   *Avnet/Hallmark*
Designer Rik Boberg
5.
Client   *GSSC*
Designer Vince Adam
6.
Client   *Caps Research*
Designer Rik Boberg
7.
Client   *Avnet/Hallmark*
Designer Joe Gunsten

opposite
Design Firm **Smith Design Associates**
Client   *Parmalat—USA*
Designer Carol Konkowski

1.

2.

3.

4.

5.

6.

7.

1
Design Firm **Spark Design**
2 - 7
Design Firm **Shook**
1.
Client   Aerial Wave
Designer   Joe Gunsten
2.
Client   Genuardi's Family Markets
Designers   Ginger Riley, Jeffrey Camillo
3.
Client   Bank of America
Designers   Ginger Riley, Jeffrey Camillo
4.
Client   Trillicom, LLC
Designers   Ginger Riley, Dave Gibson
5.
Client   SPOT'Z Gourmet Dogs &
            Frozen Custard
Designers   Ginger Riley, Jeffrey Camillo
6.
Client   Genuardi's Family Markets
Designers   Ginger Riley, Jeffrey Camillo

7.
Client   Genuardi's Family Markets
Designers   Ginger Riley, Jeffrey Camillo
opposite
Design Firm **Shook**
Client   Genuardi's Family Markets
Designers   Ginger Riley, Jeffrey Camillo

1.

The Diamond Place

2.

floor
third
the

3.

zen

4.

BEVERLY
WINE CELLAR • CIGAR DIVAN • DISCOTHEQUE

5.

StarSim

6.

RADIANCE
Communications

7.

EWi

8.

imago

9.

10.

11.

13.

14.

15.

(all)

Design Firm **Ukulele Design Consultants Pte Ltd**

1.
Client   *The Diamond Place*
Designers   Kim Chun Wei, Mr. Chadir

2.
Client   *The Pan Pacific Hotel Singapore Pte Ltd*
Designers   Kim Chun Wei, Tee Siew Lin

3.
Client   *Prime Electrical Products (Pte) Ltd*
Designers   Kim Chun Wei, Lynn Lim

4.
Client   *Beverly*
Designers   Kim Chun Wei, Mr. Chadir

5.
Client   *Giesecke & Devrient Asia Pte Ltd*
Designers   Kim Chun Wei, Mr. Chadir

6.
Client   *Radiance Communications Pte Ltd*
Designers   Kim Chun Wei, Lee Shin Kee

7.
Client   *Ewis Aste Enterprise Pte Ltd*
Designers   Kim Chun Wei, Lynn Lim

8.
Client   *Prime Electrical Products (Pte) Ltd*
Designers   Kim Chun Wei, Lynn Lim

9.
Client   *Italian Spa*
Designers   Verna Lim, Lynn Lim

10.
Client   *Reed Exhibition Pte Ltd*
Designers   Kim Chun Wei, Lynn Lim

11.
Client   *IBM Singapore Pte Ltd*
Designers   Kim Chun Wei, Lee Shin Kee

12.
Client   *Prime Electrical Products (Pte) Ltd*
Designers   Kim Chun Wei, Lynn Lim

13.
Client   *Pretty Woman*
Designers   Verna Lim, Lynn Lim

14.
Client   *J.D. Edwards (Asia Pacific) Pte Ltd*
Designers   Kim Chun Wei, Lynn Lim

15.
Client   *e-Micro Corporation*
Designers   Kim Chun Wei, Stephanie Tan

1.

SEDONA CORPORATION

2.

3.

4.

5.

6.

EDAW SSP 2000

RIDGEFIELD
NATIONAL
WILDLIFE
REFUGE

7.

1, 4, 6
Design Firm **Fixgo Advertising (M) Sdn Bhd**
2, 3
Design Firm **Communication Via Design**
5, 7
Design Firm **EDAW Graphics Studio**
1.
Client   *Omnisys dotcom*
Designers   FGA Creative Team
2.
Client   *Sedona Corporation*
Designers   Victoria Adjami, Stephen Preston
3.
Client   *Stonebridge Technology Associates*
Designers   Victoria Adjami, Stephen Preston,
    Cristine Corso
4.
Client   *Cargosave*
Designers   FGA Creative Team
5.
Client   *EDAW, Inc.*
Designer   Marty McGraw

6.
Client   *Palmshine*
Designers   FGA Creative Team
7.
Client   *EDAW, Inc.*
Designer   Marty McGraw
opposite
Design Firm **Hornall Anderson Design Works**
Client   *Space Needle*
Designers   Jack Anderson, Mary Hermes,
    Gretchen Cook, Andrew Smith,
    Julie Lock, Alan Florsheim,
    Holly Craven, Elmer Dela Cruz,
    Belinda Bowling, Amy Fawcette,
    Tyler Cartier

 DECK. 520' viewing

sky City 360' dining

SKYLINE. 100' events

S·P·A·C·E. 100% shopping

dinner

live the view

sky City

1.

2.

3.

4.

5.

6.

7.

8.

9.

MOORE'S SPORTS **EYEGEAR** FOR BASEBALL

10.

MOORE'S SPORTS **EYEGEAR** FOR GOLF

11.

Mercy Magic On Safari

12.

CKRC CEMENT KILN RECYCLING COALITION

13.

STAFF BENEFITS SERVICES

14.

HIRECHECK

15.

1 - 13
Design Firm **Arista Advertising, Inc.**
14, 15
Design Firm **Ervin Bell Advertising**

1.
Client   *Towson Orthopetic Surgi Center*
Designer   Fanny Chakedis

2.
Client   *Baltimore Reads*
Designers   Fanny Chakedis, Rebecca Stevens

3.
Client   *International Elephant Foundation*
Designers   Fanny Chakedis, Pattie Gerding

4.
Client   *The Olson Group*
Designers   David Walper, Pattie Gerding

5.
Client   *McCormick + Company*
           Health Services
Designers   David Walper, Rebecca Stevens

6.
Client   *McCormick + Company*
Designer   Fanny Chakedis

7.
Client   *Moore Sports Vision*
Designers   Fanny Chakedis, David Walper,
           Patricia Gerding

8.
Client   *Mercy Medical Center*
Designers   Patricia Gerding, Fanny Chakedis

9.
Client   *Mercy Medical Center*
Designer   Patricia Gerding

10.
Client   *Moore Sports Vision*
Designers   Fanny Chakedis, David Walper,
           Patricia Gerding

11.
Client   *Moore Sports Vision*
Designers   Fanny Chakedis, David Walper,
           Patricia Gerding

12.
Client   *Mercy Medical Center*
Designer   Fanny Chakedis

13.
Client   *Cement Kiln Recycling Coalition*
Designers   David Walper, Fanny Chakedis

14.
Client   *SBS (Staff Benefits Services)*
Designer   Jileen Hohle

15.
Client   *HireCheck*
Designer   Jileen Hohle

1.

2.

3.

4.

5.

6.

7.

1 - 5
Design Firm **Iron Design**
6, 7
Design Firm **Blank, Inc.**

1.
Client *AIDS Work of Tompkins County—*
 Ride for Life 2001
Designer Louis Johnson

2.
Client *Multi-City Technology Incubator*
Designers Todd Edmonds, Jim Keller

3.
Client *Thin Computing, Inc.—*
 Betwin Software
Designer Jim Keller

4.
Client *Avant Consulting*
Designer Jim Keller

5.
Client *Mimi Hockman*
Designer Louis Johnson

6.
Client *AssistMatch*
Designers Danielle Weller, Robert Kent Wilson

7.
Client *Coolspace*
Designers Jason Thompson,
 Robert Kent Wilson

opposite
Design Firm **Desbrow & Associates**
Client *Vocollect*
Designer Brian Lee Campbell

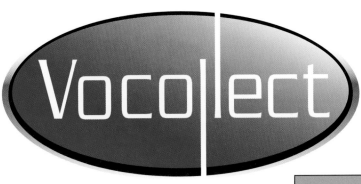

SPEED

LET'S TALK SPEED.

Need to rev up your processes

and your people? Beat the clock to

beat the competition?

Make it in a "just-in-time" world?

Let's talk Voice. Let's talk Vocollect.

At Vocollect, our business is putting voice technology to work. Making it not only possible, but immensely practical, for workers to talk to their computer systems — and have them talk back.

Talking to each other in words makes the whole work process simpler, easier, faster.

It cuts the time and effort spent on data entry. Stops errors in their tracks. Eliminates paper — and paperwork. And frees up workers' hands and eyes for the job — enabling warehouse and other floor workers to handle products and tasks in record time.

Wins that are worth shouting about.

VOICE POWERED SOLUTIONS FOR BUSINESS

Vocollect • 701 Rodi Road • Pittsburgh, PA 15235 • t) 412.829.8145 • f) 412.829.0972 • www.vocollect.com

1.

2.

3.

4.

5.

6.

7.

8.

9.

STGTA
SOUTH TEXAS GOLF
TOURNAMENT ASSOCIATION

10.

RIDE FOR YOUTH

11.

DIABLOS

13.

CREATIVE CLUB
OF SAN ANTONIO, INC.

12.

STANFORD
WRITING ASSESSMENT PROGRAM
ONLINE

14.

RANDOLPH BROOKS
SERVICES GROUP, LLC

15.

1.

2.

3.

[McELFISH + COMPANY]

5.

4.

6.

7.

1, 2, 6
Design Firm **McElveney & Palozzi Design Group**

3 - 5, 7
Design Firm **McElfish + Company**

1.
Client *Optical Gaging Products (QVS)*
Designers Lisa Williamson, Matt Nowicki

2.
Client *Highfalls Brewing Company— Michael Shea's*
Designers Jon Westfall, Mike Johnson

3.
Client *Betz Trucking*
Designer Paul Aiuto

4.
Client *Great Lakes Fabricators & Erectors Association (GLFEA)*
Designer Paul Aiuto

5.
Client *McElfish + Company*
Designer Paul Aiuto

6.
Client *Legacy Construction Corporation*
Designers Jon Westfall, Matt Dundon

7.
Client *Micropure Water Services*
Designer Paul Aiuto

opposite
Design Firm **Hornall Anderson Design Works**
Client *Ghirardelli Chocolate Company*
Designers Jack Anderson, Debra McCloskey, Darlin Gray, Jana Wilson Esser, John Anderle, Mary Chin Hutchison, Beckon Wyld, Tobi Brown, Taro Sakita, Dorothee Soechting

CRC

PANE ITALIA PTE LTD

2.

1.

D B & B

3.

heaven's **touch**

4.

MUMS BABES

5.

嘉 香 大 酒 樓

KIA HIANG
restaurant

6.

7.

Water Ventures

8.

FAMILYCLICK

9.

THE
ATRIUM
L O U N G E

10.

U K U L E L E
D E S I G N

11.

12.

Q|doz
quintessential living

13.

telesurf

14.

15.

365

1.

POLARIS

onexstream

2.

3.

ASSET | TRADE ™

4.

LaQuatra Bonci Associates

5.

PITTSBURGH
SYMPHONY

6.

PITTSBURGH SYMPHONY
BRIDGES
Education & Community Outreach

7.

1, 2, 4
Design Firm **Orbit Integrated**
3
Design Firm **Michael Lee Advertising & Design, Inc.**
5 - 7
Design Firm **Agnew Moyer Smith**
1.
Client *Polaris Consulting*
Designer Heather Meakin
2.
Client *Onexstream*
Designer Orbit Integrated
3.
Client *Southeast Texas Regional Airport*
Designer Michael Lee
4.
Client *AssetTrade*
Designer Ed Abbott
5.
Client *La Quatra Bonci Associates*
Designers John Sotirakis, Lisa Vitalbo

6.
Client *Pittsburgh Symphony*
Designer John Sotirakis
7.
Client *Pittsburgh Symphony*
Designer John Sotirakis
opposite
Design Firm **Hornall Anderson Design Works**
Client *XOW!*
Designers Jack Anderson, Lisa Cerveny, Bruce Branson-Meyer, Mary Chin Hutchison, Jana Nishi, Don Stayner

1.

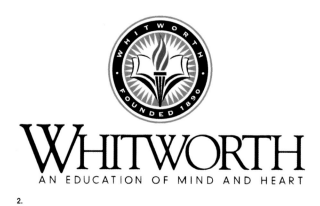

2.

3.

4.

5.

6.

7.

8.

9.

NORTHWEST
MUSEUM
OF ARTS
& CULTURE

10.

11.

WINERY

12.

13.

14.

The Human Potential Project

15.

(all)
Design Firm **Klündt Hosmer Design**
Designer   Darin Klündt

1.
  Client   *Jacob's Java*
  Designer   Brian Gage

2.
  Client   *Whitworth College*
  Designer   Brian Gage

3.
  Client   *Mead School District*
  Designer   Lorri Feenan

4.
  Client   *Enerphaze*
  Designers   Eric Grinstead, Judy Heggem-Davis

5.
  Client   *Express Theatre Northwest*
  Designer   Lorri Feenan

6.
  Client   *Alera Lighting*
  Designer   Henry Ortega

7.
  Client   *Discovery School*
  Designers   Rick Hosmer, Lorri Feenan

8.
  Client   *Damon & Magnuson*
  Designer   Diane Mahan

9.
  Client   *ProManage*
  Designer   Henry Ortega

10.
  Client   *Northwest Museum of*
               Arts and Culture
  Designers   Lorri Feenan, Brian Gage

11.
  Client   *Spokane Parks Foundation*
  Designer   Judy Heggem-Davis

12.
  Client   *Maryhill Winery*
  Designer   Judy Heggem-Davis

13.
  Client   *Webprint*
  Designer   Brian Gage

14.
  Client   *Fort Spokane Brewery*
  Designers   Judy Heggem-Davis, Eric Grinstead

15.
  Client   *The Human Potential Project*
  Designer   Lorri Feenan

1.

2.

3.

4.

5.

6.

7.

1 - 6
Design Firm **Mark Spector, Architect**
Designer Mark Spector
7
Design Firm **Stewart Monderer**
1.
Client *Miami PC*
2.
Client *Alternative Treatment*
3.
Client *Brittex*
4.
Client *Mueller and Associates*
5.
Client *Shelly Development Corp.*
6.
Client *Hackett's*
7.
Client *Sockeye Networks, Inc.*
Designers Jeffrey Gobin, Stewart Monderer

opposite
Design Firm **Muts & Joy & Inc.**
Client *Banfi Vintners (Concha y Toro)*
Designers Tom Delaney, Akira Otani,
Gisele Sangiovanni

EST. 1883

CONCHA y TORO

BEECHWOOD WINES

GOULBURN VALLEY

1.

Gardening Getaways™

—a gloves-on experience

2.

TRUE **MARTIAL** ARTS

FAMILY KARATE SCHOOLS

3.

PRINTING INDUSTRIES ASSOC.

Serious Hackers

SINCE 1935

GOLFING SOCIETY

4.

swinburne
university hospital

5.

SpAN
communication

6.

blackwood
studios

7.

8.

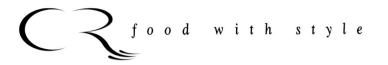 *food with style*

9.

10.

11.

12.

digital **i**nteractive **g**roup

13.

14.

15.

1, 4 - 9, 11, 14, 15
Design Firm **Watts Design**
2, 3, 10, 12, 13
Design Firm **Hansen Design Company**
Designers Pat Hansen, Jacqueline Smith

1.
Client *Beechwood Wines*
Designer Peter Watts

2.
Client *Gardening Getaways*

3.
Client *True Martial Arts*

4.
Client *Printing Industry Golfing Society*
Designer Peter Watts

5.
Client *Swinburne University Hospital*
Designers Peter Watts, Helen Watts

6.
Client *Span Communication*
Designer David Fry

7.
Client *Blackwood Studios*
Designer Peter Watts

8.
Client *Healesville Sanctuary*
Designer Linda Ho

9.
Client *Carol Rieley*
Designer David Fry

10.
Client *Gibbons Lane Winery*

11.
Client *Amway Australia*
Designer Helen Watts

12.
Client *Family Services*

13.
Client *Digital Interactive Group*

14.
Client *Darriwill Farm*
Designer Peter Watts

15.
Client *World Amateur Putting Challenge*
Designer Peter Watts

1.

2.

3.

4.

5.

6.

7.

1 - 7
Design Firm **Mark Spector, Architect**
Designer   Mark Spector

1.
Client   *Copperwood*

2.
Client   *Barstools and More*

3.
Client   *Rosi Vergara*

4.
Client   *Jonida International*

5.
Client   *Shelly Katz*

6.
Client   *Logan Lilly*

7.
Client   *Spector Builders*

opposite
Design Firm **Orbit Integrated**
Client   *Jack Harris*
Designer   Mark Miller

374

722 Yorklyn Road
Suite 150, Hockessin, DE 19707

v 302-477-1689 | 1-888-241-3103
f 302-477-1684

e jack.harris@jackharris.com
i www.jackharris.com

722 Yorklyn Road
Suite 150, Hockessin, DE 19707

v 302-477-1689 | 1-888-241-3103
f 302-477-1684

e jack.harris@jackharris.com
i www.jackharris.com

1.

Saint Peter Claver Church
A DIVERSE SPIRITUAL
COMMUNITY IN ACTION

2.

Wine Valet

3.

4.

5.

market
JAZZ

Buy, sell and all that jazz

6.

skyriver℠
How Broadband Flows

7.

STARLIGHT
THEATRE

8.

TIMESHARE SOURCE

9.

10.

11.

12.

13.

Expertise for growth. SM

14.

CALIFORNIA
BENTO
QUICK HEALTHY FOOD

15.

1, 2
   Design Firm **Smith Design Associates**
3 - 5, 8, 11 - 13
   Design Firm **CWA, Inc.**
6, 7, 9, 10, 14, 15
   Design Firm **Crouch and Naegeli/**
               Design Group West

1.
   Client   *Global Village*
   Designers James Smith, Keith Druckenmiller
2.
   Client   *Saint Peter Claver R.C. Church*
   Designers James Smith, Eileen Berezni
3.
   Client   *R.S. Ellis and Sons*
   Designers Bryan Montgomery, Randy Moyer
4.
   Client   *Asian American Journalists*
              Association of San Diego
   Designer   Marco Sipriaso
5.
   Client   *Nine Dragons, Inc.*
   Designer   Scott Wyss
6.
   Client   *Market Jazz*
   Designer   Jim Naegeli

7.
   Client   *Skyriver*
   Designers Jim Crouch, Aleta Reese
8.
   Client   *Starlight Theatre*
   Designers Chris Burris, Scott Wyss
9.
   Client   *Timeshare Source*
   Designer   Jim Naegeli
10.
   Client   *Openfirst*
   Designer   Jim Naegeli
11.
   Client   *San Diego World Trade Center*
   Designer   Scott Wyss
12.
   Client   *The McMillin Development Co.*
   Designer   Marco Sipriaso
13.
   Client   *San Diego Police Department*
   Designer   Marco Sipriaso
14.
   Client   *e stockoptions*
   Designer   Jim Naegeli
15.
   Client   *Bento*
   Designer   Jim Naegeli

3.

4.

5.

1, 2, 5
Design Firm **Phil Meilinger**
3, 4, 6, 7
Design Firm **Pollman Marketing Arts, Inc.**
1.
Client   *Blue Ridge Lawn & Garden*
2.
Client   *Cristo Rey Jesuit High School*
3.
Client   *Association Partners Plus*
Designers Jennifer Pollman, Erin Trice
4.
Client   *Center for Executive Leadership*
Designers Jennifer Pollman, Erin Trice
5.
Client   *Blue Frog Beads*
6.
Client   *Lynott & Associates*
Designers Jennifer Pollman, Erin Trice
7.
Client   *Dayton Land and Real Estate*
Designers Jennifer Pollman, Erin Trice

opposite
Design Firm **Hornall Anderson Design Works**
Client   *Widmer Brothers*
Designers Jack Anderson, Larry Anderson,
           Bruce Stigler, Bruce Branson-Meyer,
           Mary Chin Hutchison, Kaye Farmer,
           Ed Lee, Michael Brugman

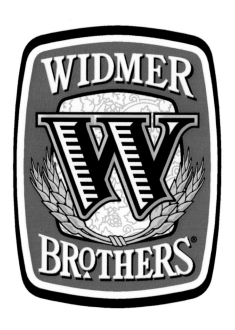
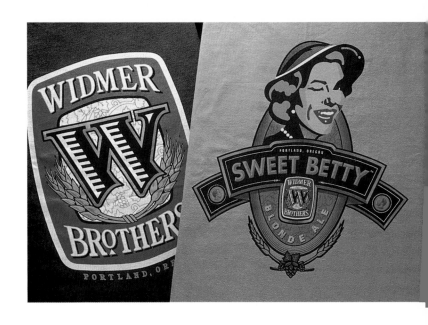

INDEX
Design Firms

Clients

384